THE
TILE
BOOK

THE
TILE
BOOK

HISTORY · PATTERN · DESIGN

INTRODUCTION BY TERRY BLOXHAM

  Thames & Hudson | **V&A**

V&A Publishing
Supporting the world's leading museum of art and design, the Victoria and Albert Museum, London

INTRODUCTION

On entering the Imam Mosque in Isfahan (p.18), the visitor is over-whelmed by the brilliance of the blue tiles. Almost half a million tiles reflect and absorb light and the concentric pattern of the tiled dome interior creates a sense of heavenly transcendence. The dome's exterior is also tiled. This is a distinct feature of Islamic architecture in Central Asia and Iran, and foreign traders following the Silk Road would have seen such domes from miles away, glinting in the sunlight.

The Imam Mosque is just one example of how the story of tiles is inseparable from the history of place, politics, economics and culture, including the development of architecture, design and ceramics. The simplicity of the individual tile form partly accounts for the tradition of tile-making lasting for more than three millennia. It has also meant that the techniques of today are not dissimilar to those that were used in pharaonic Egypt, where the earliest archaeological evidence of tiles has been found. Cut from a slab of clay, or shaped in a mould, the tile is fired in a kiln and then glazed or left unglazed. Glazed tiles are less porous and easier to clean, and were used by the ancient Egyptians to decorate the subterranean chambers of the Step Pyramid at Saqqara, in greenish-blue. Unglazed tiles proved particularly useful in the Roman Empire: the Romans kept their rooms warm by paving their floors with unglazed tiles, which absorbed heat from the hypocaust systems beneath.

Opposite A series of tiles forming a decorative frieze made for the Gamble Room, part of the Victoria and Albert Museum's café, featuring an illustrated alphabet designed by Godfrey Sykes (1824–1866). Minton, Hollins & Co, Stoke-on-Trent, England, 1867–9 (see also p.15)

Tiles are found in many shapes – irregular or regular: square, round, diamond, rectangular, trapezoid, hexagonal, cruciform or star-shaped – as seen in this book. From the illustrative to the abstract, the possibility of design, pattern and colour is endless. Some tiles bear self-contained motifs, such as the famous blue-and-white Delft tiles (pp.144–5), with picturesque scenes of 18th-century Dutch towns. Others do not reveal their grand design until fully laid out, like components of a jigsaw puzzle, such as the Syrian 16th- and 17th-century tiles on pp.108–11, which were perhaps inspired by a real palatial garden, abundant with flowers, pots and peacocks. *The Tile Book* presents an extraordinary range of tiles with their many different functions, and visually unravels the history of tiles from the 13th century to the present day.

Although the great churches and monasteries in Europe commissioned tiled flooring prior to the 13th century, it is in that century that we see an increase in royal and upper aristocratic commissions in northern Europe. Tiles were primarily standardized square shapes but more complicated, and hence more expensive, flooring incorporated rounded shapes. Designs were stamped into these shapes and filled in with a different coloured clay. Red earthenware was the most commonly used base clay and the stamped design was filled in with white clay in either plastic (solid) or slip (watered-down clay) form. A single design could be stamped into each tile, the combination of which could form an array of heraldic devices or scenes from popular stories (pp.28–9 and 32–5). Equally, each tile could be stamped with an element of a multipart pattern (pp.30–1). These stamped (patterned) tiles would be arranged with plain or coloured glazed tiles of different shapes to form a decorative floor. This type of flooring prevailed in northern Europe until the 16th century when a new technique, introduced from the Middle East and popular in southern Europe in the Middle Ages, began to appear.

The technique of painting designs onto a tin-opacified lead glaze was transmitted along the Mediterranean trade routes from Iran, into the Near East and then to the West via the Iberian peninsula and Italy. Initially, square tiles of white clay formed into complex painted patterns appeared in southern France (pp.44–5). By the end of the 15th century, more complex tiled patterns were formed using painted tin-glazed hexagons surrounding squares that often bore painted armorials, as seen in the fine clay-tile pavements of southern Spain and Italy (pp.62–5).

Combining different tile shapes to form elaborate geometric patterns had been practised in the Middle East for centuries and is beautifully exemplified in the cutwork panels from a tomb in Uzbekistan (pp.50–1). Islamic secular and religious buildings were ornamented extensively with decorative brick and tile work. Complex geometric patterns, composed of combinations of star, cross, square and lozenge shapes, were used to spectacular effect to cover whole interior walls and ceilings and exterior surfaces. Lustre, a technique first developed in the Middle East, was a popular decoration on eight-pointed star shapes, and was often combined with cross shapes and painted with floral, arabesque and figurative forms as seen in the 14th-century tiles from Kashan in modern-day Iran (pp.52–7). We also see tiles moulded in relief with inscriptions from the Qur'an or shaped into the form of *mihrabs* (prayer niches; pp.46–9).

In the 16th century new design sources appeared in Europe and were disseminated widely through mass-produced prints. The remains of Emperor Nero's palace, built in the 1st century CE and described as his grotto, were rediscovered in Rome at the end of the 15th century. Large areas of painted wall plaster were revealed, and their designs eagerly recorded by visiting artists. Stylized foliate decoration and hybrid creatures, termed 'grotesques' by contemporaries, soon came into the decorative vocabulary of tile decorators in the West as exemplified in the tiling of the Petrucci Palace in Siena (pp.68–71), the geometric floor made in Forlì in central Italy (pp.72–3), and the flooring in Anne de Montmorency's château at Écouen in northern France (pp.74–5). Tile-making in Spain had developed under an Islamic caliphate and reflected Middle Eastern geometric models, but makers also began to adopt the current mode for grotesques and Neoclassical forms (pp.82–7). In central Europe, tiled stoves become more commonplace; these were composed of coloured lead-glaze tiles moulded in relief with images from the Bible and classical mythology (pp.90–3). The colours were derived from mineral oxides. Using copper, cobalt, manganese, iron and antimony, they produced a range of rich, glossy colours.

The Mughal Empire, established in the Indian subcontinent in the early decades of the 16th century, spread the Islamic tradition of decorative tile work. Soon, native Indian classical foliate forms were incorporated into the decoration along with new techniques of relief-moulding (pp.76–9). Iznik, in Turkey, began to produce on a large scale its distinctive fritware coloured with blue, green and red on a white-slip coating, alongside hexagonal tiles painted in underglaze blue and turquoise, which were also produced in workshops in Damascus, Syria (pp.94–103). The beautiful turquoise glazed painted panel on pp.104–5 is decorated with representations of tiger stripes, a motif that was popular in Ottoman Turkey before spreading to other centres of production in the Islamic world.

Italian tile makers brought the art of painted tin-glazed tilework to the Low Countries (the Netherlands) in the 16th century, and in the following century this technique was used to great effect on wall tiles, incorporating both Spanish geometric and Italian Renaissance motifs. Tile painters employed printed sources for their hand-painted composite panels consisting of fruit, floral and animal patterns (pp.124–9). By the end of the century, many of the decorated tiles produced in the Low Countries were painted solely in either manganese-purple or cobalt-blue pigment on a white tin-glazed ground. Blue painted onto white tiles was popular due to the influence of the Ming Dynasty blue-on-white porcelain, which the Dutch East Indies Company traders brought in huge quantities from China to the West. Subject matter included contemporary scenes such as the Rotterdam panel of a whaling ship (pp.136–7) and events that had captured the popular imagination. The Popish Plot, a fabricated conspiracy against the English king Charles II, was a series made by Dutch tile makers established in London who copied the images from Popish Plot playing cards (p.132). The Dutch were prolific tile makers, producing works for export as seen in a tile depicting Charles II (p.133). The popular painted tin-glaze technique was adopted for decorated tiled stoves with panels illustrating scenes from the Bible, history, mythology and moralizing texts as illustrated by a tile that warns against bad behaviour (p.130).

The natural world was a popular theme in the Near East as seen in the beautiful 17th-century panels from Damascus which depict stylized floral displays in calming shades of blue, green and turquoise (pp.108–13). The two early 17th-century panels depicting dancers (pp.114–15) are thought to have adorned the baths of a palace in Safavid Iran. Their pose and the colours used prefigure the western Art Nouveau period of the late 19th and early 20th centuries. Mughal Empire buildings in what is now modern India were adorned with brightly coloured tiles painted with arabesques and floral displays, executed in the *cuerda seca* technique (pp.118–23).

Blue-and-white and manganese-purple painted tin-glazed tiles remained in fashion into the 18th century and reflected the tastes of a widening consumer market. The panel with its scene of wealthy men and women enjoying music in a garden (pp.140–1) is said to have adorned the walls of the Music Room of the Quinta Formosa in Lisbon, Portugal. The tiles featuring scenes from the Bible painted in purple and the tiles of local views set in octagons painted in blue would have come from a humbler, yet prosperous, domestic setting in the Netherlands (pp.142–4). Dutch canvas painters' fascination for colourful floral displays crossed over into the painted-tile industry (pp.146–7). As mechanization began to be introduced into agriculture and other industries, a nostalgia for the crafts of the past became evident, as seen in the brightly coloured tiles depicting traditional skills in Catalonia in Spain (pp.148–9). However, new processes applied to tile-decorating dramatically cut the costs of what had been a labour-intensive industry. Transfer-printing, a British invention, enabled images to be mass-reproduced onto simple white, tin-glazed tile surfaces. Manufacturers such as Sadler & Green of Liverpool copied contemporary prints of popular actors and actresses onto their fireplace and wall tiles. Equally, nostalgic scenes of rural life and classical images familiar to those who had gone on a Grand Tour were bestsellers (pp.152–5). Marbleizing, a technique by which coloured slips and glazes are added and swirled onto ceramic tiles, was also popular in the Netherlands and England (pp.156–9).

The latter part of the 18th century witnessed the beginnings of what would become known as the Gothic Revival in the 19th century. In Europe and in North America, designers, architects and manufacturers were becoming interested in the surviving material culture of the Middle Ages. The English architect and designer A.W.N. Pugin (1812–52) copied patterns from medieval tiles found during excavations and restorations of religious and domestic buildings and worked with ceramic manufacturers such as Minton & Co. in Stoke-on-Trent to reproduce the designs. Herbert Minton (1793–1858) successfully resurrected the medieval technique of floor-tile production, forming standardized shapes with primarily red clay and stamping them with a design that was then infilled with white or coloured clays. The huge demand for these Gothic Revival floors led other manufacturers to set up or turn their business over to floor- and wall-tile production (pp.166–81). The invention of the dust-pressed method of tile-making dramatically reduced the costs of production and with the new technique of block-printing, also in use by the 1860s, manufacturers could recreate the look of an inlaid tile without the labour-intensive technique of stamping and inlaying.

The Great Exhibition in London's Hyde Park in 1851 was the first of many such events that gave international manufacturers the opportunity to display their products, including tiles. Using a variety of machine-assisted methods such as dust-pressing, printing and stencilling, these manufacturers offered their tiles to the public to both admire and purchase. Many of the designs and patterns displayed were inspired by the past, borrowing from diverse cultural traditions, and were influenced by the illustrations in Owen Jones's *The Grammar of Ornament*, published in 1856 as an essential reference book for artists and designers. The printed, painted and moulded tiles on pp.182–9 show a range of historic designs – classical, Persian, Hispano-Moresque. One of the exhibitors at the Great Exhibition was Rafael Gonzalez Valls of Valencia in Spain. His patterns are large, bold and colourful and are best understood when seen as an interlocking pattern of decorated tiles (pp.190–9).

The British artist and designer William Morris (1834–96) was fascinated with the Middle Ages and, in reaction to widespread mechanization, set up a business that he believed resurrected the skills of the medieval artist–craftsman. In the 1860s Morris designed a variety of foliate patterns to be hand-painted onto domestic fireplace and wall tiles. He contracted artists such as William De Morgan (1839–1917) to execute his designs. De Morgan later set up his own ceramic production in London, making hand-made tiles, but he also used imported dust-pressed tiles from the Netherlands to execute Morris's designs. Additionally, De Morgan reintroduced the technique of lustre, hand-painting his designs onto his tiles using metallic oxides (pp.200–11).

Narrative tiles were popular in both the West and the Middle East at the end of the 19th century. The Grill Room at the Victoria and Albert Museum features wall panels depicting the seasons designed by Edward Poynter (1836–1919) and executed by female art students (pp.216–19). Scenes from popular writings such as the epic poems *Khamsa of Nizami* and *Shahnameh* were produced in Iran for both a domestic and a tourist market (pp.220–5). Equally, tiles with scenes from Shakespeare's plays and Aesop's fables, personifications of flowers and humorous depictions of children playing at work were ordered in large numbers for various rooms in middle-class homes (pp.230–8).

The early 20th century was characterized by two dominant artistic movements in Europe and America: Art Nouveau and Art Deco. By this time, tile manufacturers were producing standardized plain tiles in huge numbers and contracting contemporary artists, such as Walter Crane (1845–1915) and C.F.A. Voysey (1857–1941), to create designs that were then executed by skilled craftsmen. Tube-lining by hand creates a beautiful effect but was labour-intensive as it involved 'drawing' the design with slip by hand (pp.244–5 and p.247). Moulds used to create the raised slip lines brought costs down (pp.242–3 and p.246). After the First World War some artists in Britain reacted against this mechanization and created more hand-worked tiles, such as the painted tin-glazed tiles by Vanessa Bell (1879–1961) and Duncan Grant (1885–1978; pp.252–3). Bernard Leach (1887–1979), one of Britain's greatest ceramicists, exploited the natural textures of clay and painted simple designs inspired by nature (p.258). His work influenced later tile makers such as Heber Mathews (*c*.1907–1959; p.259).

Mechanization meant that affordable tiles could be produced on a large scale for public commissions like the Carter & Co. tiles designed for London Transport (pp.256–7). Carter & Co. continued to work with artists after the Second World War, replicating their designs by silk-screening onto standard dust-pressed square tiles in order to satisfy a much larger buying public. The artist Peggy Angus (1904–93), notably, was a prolific designer for the firm. Angus produced linocuts of simple flat designs, often taken from potato prints she had created for her students. These designs created a powerful effect when covering large expanses of walling (pp.260–3 and pp.273–4).

The 1960s and 1970s can be seen as an age of pushing boundaries in design in the West. Irregular forms and colours produced with special glazes were applied to standard mass-produced tiles to create new and exciting patterns for decorating walls (pp.275–81). At the same time, tile designers continued to be influenced by earlier styles and artists. The contemporary artist Sally Anderson was inspired by Art Nouveau and particularly by the pattern work of the artist–designer Reginald Till (1895–1978) whose 'coloured-line tiles' were incorporated in Carter, Stabler & Adams Pottery's tearoom in Poole, Dorset, 1932 (pp.282–7).

The tiles in this book have been selected from the vast collection of the Victoria and Albert Museum, London, to reveal the remarkable variety and the shared design vocabulary used over time and between cultures. Through generous gifts and judicious purchases from specialist collectors, the Museum has acquired an impressive collection of tiles from many of the world's most notable tile-making traditions. When leafing through *The Tile Book*, it is easy to understand why tiles and tile-making have endured for so long. Apart from their usefulness, durability and relative ease of production, it is their decorative aspect that unites them, and the universal desire to personalize our surroundings.

Opposite A series of tiles forming a decorative frieze made for the Gamble Room, part of the Victoria and Albert Museum's café, featuring an illustrated alphabet designed by Godfrey Sykes (1824–66). Minton, Hollins & Co, Stoke-on-Trent, England, 1867–9

CARMELO

ECCE SIGNUM SALUTIS
SALUS IN PERICULIS

Cosmati Pavement, Westminster Abbey, London, England, 1268 (p.16)

King Henry III commissioned this remarkable pavement for Westminster Abbey in the mid-13th century. It was constructed by workers from Rome and its name derives from a form of inlaid stone decoration known as Cosmati work. The pavement is made up of multicoloured stones, including onyx, purple porphyry, green serpentine and yellow limestone, as well as coloured glass cut into a variety of shapes and sizes. The basic design is a four-fold symmetry but each infill pattern is unique.

La Casa de Pilatos, Seville, Spain, late 15th to early 16th century (p.17)

The palace of La Casa de Pilatos in Seville, so-called as it was thought to resemble Pontius Pilate's home in Jerusalem, blends Renaissance architecture with Islamic elements. It includes over 150 different tile designs typical of the 16th century. The Seville workshop of the Pulido family made 2000 tiles a week for the refurbishment in 1538, resulting in one of the largest tiled surfaces of the time.

Main entranceway to the Imam Mosque, Isfahan, Iran, 1612 (p.18)

Constructed as the architectural jewel of the Persian capital, which moved to Isfahan in the early 17th century, the huge Imam Mosque is decorated internally and externally with predominately blue 'seven-colour' tiles. The main entrance gateway has a recessed arch with stunningly complex tilework *muqarnas* – a form of ornamental vaulting sometimes known as honeycomb or stalactite vaulting which, as one looks heavenwards, symbolically

represents the vast complexity of universal creation.

Cloister Garden, Santa Chiara Monastery, Naples, Italy, 1742 (p.19)

The monastic complex of Santa Chiara was built in the early to mid-13th century. The original church was redecorated in the Baroque style by Domenico Antonio Vaccaro (1678–1745) during the 18th century, famously transforming the cloister with the addition of colourful maiolica tiles. The tiles are hand-painted with rural and maritime scenes bordered by vines of blue and yellow flowers, lemons and grapes.

The Arab Hall, Leighton House, London, England, c.1877–9 (p.20)

Built in stages from 1865, Leighton House was the home of artist and Royal Academy president Frederic, Lord Leighton (1830–1896). Built by George Aitchison, the Arab Hall houses Leighton's collection of 16th- and 17th-century Syrian and Iranian tiles. These were laid out by William De Morgan (1839–1917), who also manufactured reproductions to fill the gaps in the designs, caused by breakages in the shipment from Damascus.

The Gamble Room, Victoria and Albert Museum, London, England, 1868 (p.21)

The Gamble Room, designed by Geoffrey Sykes (1824–1866) and completed by James Gamble (1837–1911), was one of three refreshment rooms opened in 1868 at the South Kensington Museum (now the Victoria and Albert Museum). It was the first museum to offer a café or restaurant. The wall tiles, majolica column cladding and friezes are by Minton & Co.

Igreja do Carmo, Porto, Portugal, 1756–68; tiled exterior 1912 (p.22)

The Igreja do Carmo was built in the mid-18th century to house an order of Carmelite monks. In 1912, an exterior wall was decorated with an impressive panel of blue and white *azulejos* designed by the artist Silvestro Silvestri. Made locally in Vila Nova de Gaia, the painted tiles depict the 12th-century founding of the Carmelite Order on Mount Carmel in Israel.

Casa Vicens, Barcelona, Spain, 1883–5 (p.23)

Casa Vicens was the first building constructed by Antoni Gaudí (1852–1926), whose highly individual architectural and decorative style is associated with Catalan Modernism. The exterior of stone and ornate brickwork is decorated with a chequerboard combination of plain and decorated tiles featuring the iconic marigold and dianthus motifs Gaudí designed specifically for the site.

Eastern Columbia Building, Los Angeles, CA, United States, 1930 (p.25)

Known for its striking turquoise façade and four-sided clock tower, this Art Deco building was designed by Claud Beelman (1883–1963) and opened in 1930 as the new headquarters of the Eastern-Columbia Department Store. The steel and concrete building is clad in glossy ceramic tiles trimmed in deep blue and gold, and embellished with sunburst, zig-zag, chevron and stylized animal and plant motifs.

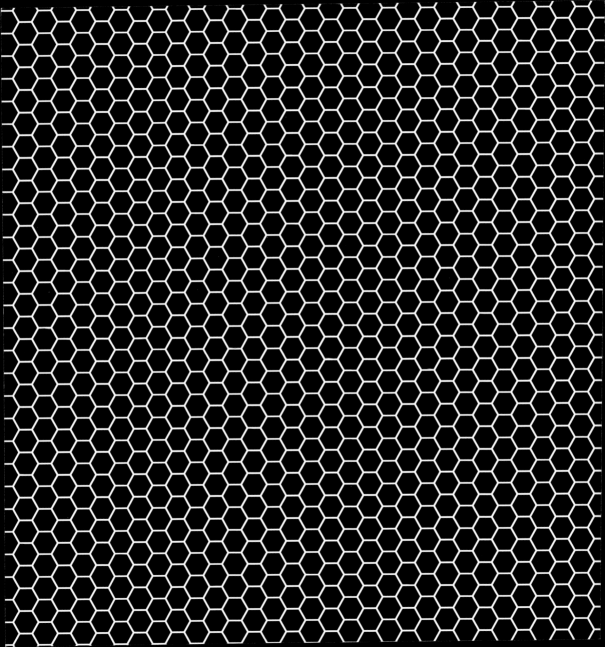

13th to 15th Century

Previous pages Shortly after his marriage to Eleanor of Provence in 1236, King Henry III of England commissioned tiled floors for Clarendon Palace, near Salisbury in Wiltshire. This new French fashion soon spread and the itinerant tile makers used the Clarendon designs of griffins, lions and fleurs-de-lys in other wealthy royal and religious centres in the south-west. This pavement is from Keynsham Abbey in Somerset. England, *c*.1250–70

Above and opposite This set of 16 red earthenware floor tiles with an inlaid design of a quatrefoil within a circle and embellished with Gothic foliage was probably produced at a Nottingham workshop for Ulverscroft Priory in Leicestershire, England. The popularity of the inlaid tile and its suitability for mass production led to the establishment of commercial tileries in the 14th century. England, 14th or 15th century

Overleaf These tile roundels depict scenes from the courtly romance of Tristan and Iseult (left) and the heroic tale of Samson and the Lion (right); both are more suited to a royal court than to an abbey. It is likely that they were commissioned for Chertsey Abbey, Surrey, by its royal patron, King Henry III. England, late 13th century

Previous pages These wall tiles are said to be from Tring Church in Hertfordshire and illustrate scenes from the infancy of Jesus Christ. An example of the *sgraffito* technique, the design is carved out of the white slip covering the red earthenware tile – a refinement unsuited to large-scale manufacture. England, *c.*1330

Opposite In the 14th century, the major tilery at Penn in Buckinghamshire supplied churches and important buildings primarily along the Thames Valley and in London with roof and floor tiles. This red earthenware example inlaid with a rabbit and Gothic foliate motifs is from Reading Abbey in Berkshire. England, *c.*1332–50

Above The double-headed eagle on this inlaid red earthenware tile is the emblem of King Henry III's brother, Richard of Cornwall. The design was also produced to celebrate the marriage of Richard's son, Edmund of Cornwall, to Margaret de Clare in 1271. Lyme Regis, Dorset, England, *c.*1270–1300

In the early decades of the 13th century, a new type of flooring developed in central and northern Frankish lands. Consisting primarily of square and rectangular inlaid tiles, this flooring also incorporated variations using a combination of slips and coloured glazes. The tile above is covered with a white slip and is divided diagonally, with one half glazed green with a copper-enriched glaze. Probably France, 14th century

This tile has been stamped with a complicated chequer
pattern of triangles, alternately filled with a white slip.
Troyes, France, late 13th or early 14th century

Above In central Europe, inlaid tiles were much less popular than the line-impressed and relief tiles that were used on walls, floors and sometimes ceilings. They were typically decorated with bold, linear geometric designs as well as figurative and fantastic imagery like these tiles from various sites: Strasbourg, France (top left); Mainz, Germany (top centre); Germany or Switzerland (top right and bottom row), late 13th or early 14th century

Opposite Tiles with decoration in high relief are also known from sites across the Alsace region of France from the 12th century onwards, such as this octagonal tile. It comes from the Church of St Faith's in Sélestat, Alsace, and depicts a knightly centaur bearing a shield and sword. Some tiles like this may have been moulded, but the standard technique involved stamping the tile with a carved wooden block. Sélestat, France, *c.*1150–80

Above Tiles with floral and fleurs-de-lys designs incorporated within a geometric framework were popular throughout medieval Europe. A variety of styles could be produced using different techniques. The tiles from the Abbey of Escaladieu in the Hautes-Pyrénées (top) are made by painting on a tin-opacified glaze, and those from Croyland Abbey, Northamptonshire (bottom left), and Langdon Abbey, Kent (bottom right), are made by impressing in relief and by inlaying. (Top) France, late 13th or early 14th century; (bottom) England, 14th century

Opposite The tile is covered with white slip, the design having first been marked out with a stencil. Troyes, France, late 13th or early 14th century

Above and opposite This group of floor tiles from the Church of St Julien, Brioude, is one of the earliest known example of painted tin-glazed tiles in France. Tin-glazed tiles such as these were produced in southern France, where inlaid tiles were rare, from the mid-13th century.

The design is painted in green and purple on a white ground and features a heraldic shield set obliquely within a circle, surrounded by stiff Gothic foliage and enclosed within a large quatrefoil. Brioude, France, 1250–1300

Opposite While this tile represents a *mihrab*, the niche in the wall of a mosque marking the *qibla* (direction of prayer), it is actually part of a tomb. The *mihrab* motif indicates that the dead should be buried facing the *qibla*, to rise facing the direction of prayer on the Day of Judgment. Probably Kashan, Iran, c.1305

Above This section of a *mihrab* with Qur'anic inscriptions and spiralling scrollwork is from the tomb of Shaykh 'Abd al-Samad in Natanz in central Iran. It is formed of monumental fritware tiles glazed in cobalt blue, turquoise and a lustre pigment. Probably Kashan, Iran, 1307–8

Above Part of a frieze from the tomb of Shaykh 'Abd al-Samad, this fritware tile with a cobalt-blue glaze with lustre pigments bears a quotation from the Qur'an. The defacement of the birds is indicative of the variety of attitudes towards figural representation in Islamic religious settings. Probably Kashan, Iran, 1307–8

Right This moulded frieze tile from the Ilkhanid Palace at Takht-i Sulayman in north-west Iran depicts the story of the Sasanian king Bahram Gur and his harpist Azadeh. While out hunting, Azadeh challenges Bahram Gur to pin together the ear and hoof of a deer with a single arrow. Probably Kashan, Iran, *c.*1275

Opposite Excerpts from the Qur'an in calligraphic script in cobalt blue over a background of intertwined foliage decorate this lustre-painted, moulded fritware tile. Running bidirectionally, the vertical letters of the bottom and middle band of letters are conjoined at the centre by symmetrical knots. Probably Kashan, Iran, 1250–1350

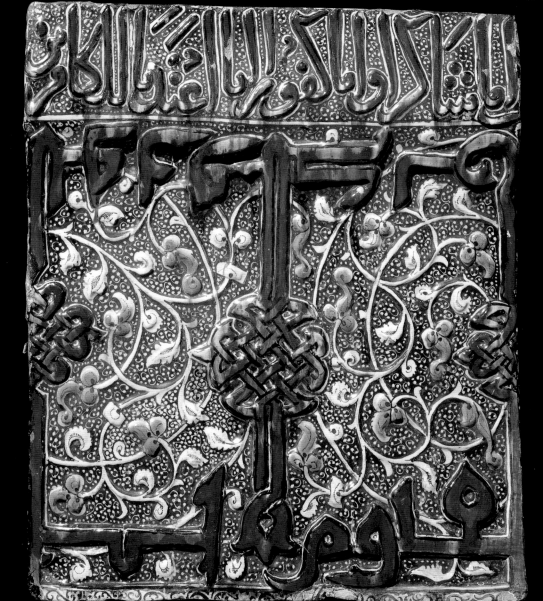

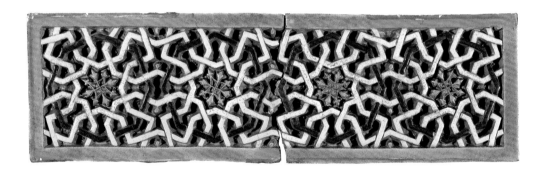

Opposite and above The magnificent, domed tomb of Buyanquli Khan, a ruler of Samarkand (modern-day Uzbekistan), assassinated in the mid-14th century, was decorated with tiles inside and out. These three earthenware panels have been deeply carved with repeating geometric patterns and covered with coloured glazes before the final firing. A restricted palette of black, white, cobalt and aubergine details on a deep turquoise blue background creates a powerful, unifying effect. This impressive technique was used in Central Asia only for a brief period, from around 1350 to the early 15th century. Bukhara, Uzbekistan, *c*.1358

The central decoration of this star-shaped tile shows
the Mongol imperial phoenix in flight, originally a secular,
figurative image highlighting the cultural impact of
Mongolian conquest on parts of Asia. The moulded
fritware tile is glazed and painted with lustre and framed
by a quotation from the Qur'an. Probably from a religious
shrine or building. Probably Kashan, Iran, 1275–1375

Above From a star and cross panel, these two fritware tiles have been enamelled and gilded with delicate foliage patterns over a dark blue and turquoise background. This style of decoration is called the lajvardina technique, a term that refers to lapis lazuli, a deep-blue coloured stone containing golden particles. Probably Kashan, Iran, early 14th century

Overleaf This panel of star and cross tiles is from the shrine of Imamzadeh Yahya in Varamin, Iran. Fritware with overglaze lustre decoration, the foliate design on every tile is subtly different, each bordered by quotations from the Qur'an. Probably Kashan, Iran, 1262

Above and opposite The designs on these eight-pointed star tiles, probably from shrines, range from delicate leaf forms and complex geometric motifs to various figurative representations, including an elephant, a brilliant blue Cypress tree flanked by two hares and a representation of a sacred Hindu bull amid floral scrollwork. The seven individual tiles are all glazed fritware, with painted lustre decoration. Kashan, Iran, late 13th or early 14th century

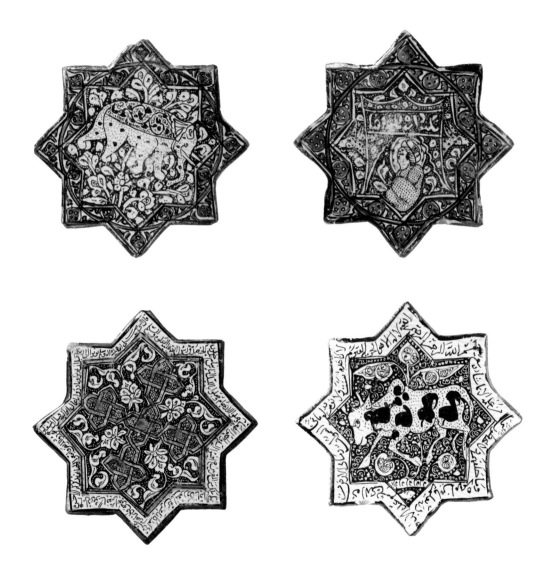

Previous pages The interspaces between the 15 clear-glazed star-shaped tiles painted with inscriptions or leaf sprays are filled with 25 green-glazed lozenges in this fritware tile panel from a shrine or a mosque. Each star tile bears a short religious phrase such as 'O God!' and 'By the Power and the Glory' written in cobalt pigment on the white ground before firing. Probably Amol, Iran, 1496–7

Above and opposite These fritware tiles made in Damascus in the first half of the 15th century highlight the cultural impact of Chinese ceramics: the cobalt-blue underglaze painted on white ground imitates the colour scheme of ceramics of the Yuan and Ming dynasties. Such patterned tiles are often interspersed with plain turquoise tiles. Damascus, Syria, 1400–50

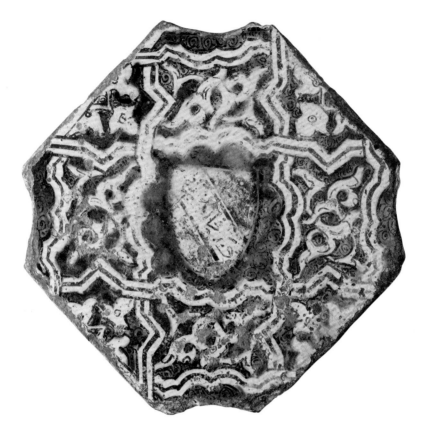

Above A tin-glazed earthenware floor tile, painted in cobalt blue and lustre, from the Alhambra, the fortified palatine city of the Nasrid Kingdom of Granada. A small circular tile would have been laid at each rounded corner, set between the larger floor tiles. Malaga or Granada, Spain, 1350–1400

Opposite This later group of Spanish tin-glazed tiles bears a clear relationship to the earlier Alhambra tile (above). Four hexagonal tiles, or alfardons, painted in cobalt blue with pious inscriptions and floral ornament are set around a central square tile with a heraldic eagle motif. Probably Manises, Valencia, 1400–50

Overleaf Decorated with Gothic peacock-feather and foliage designs, this is an early example of Italian Renaissance tiled flooring from the Church of Santa Maria della Verita, Viterbo, and is based on the layout of repeating hexaganol tiles surrounding a square as seen in the Valencian example opposite. They are painted in dark blue, manganese-purple, deep yellow and green on a tin-glazed earthenware ground. Italy, c.1470

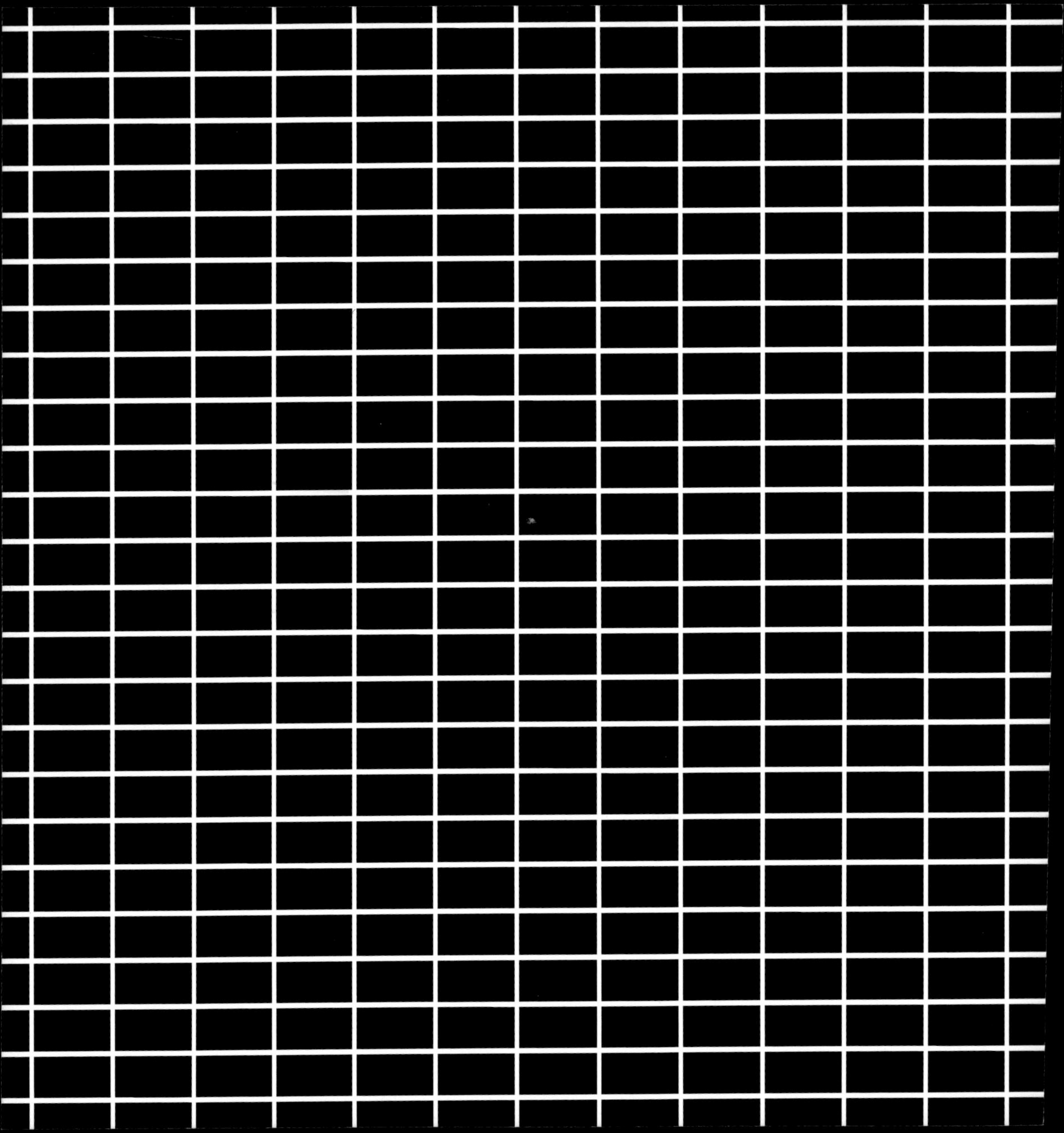

16th Century

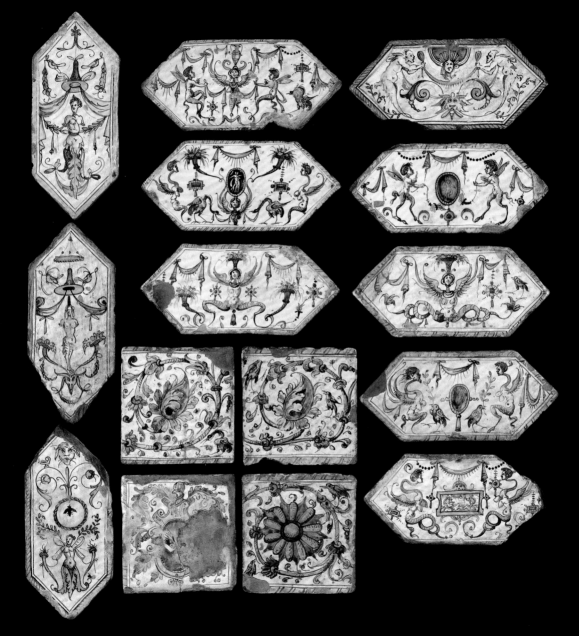

Previous pages These maiolica tiles came from the Petrucci Palace in Siena and were most likely later replacements for the original damaged floor tiles. Painted in colours on a white tin-glazed ground with floral scrolls and grotesques, these are an example of the later 16th-century fashion for light rather than dark backgrounds. Faenza, Italy, late 16th century

Above and opposite These maiolica tiles come from an original pavement in the Petrucci Palace, Siena, commissioned in 1509 to celebrate the union of the Petrucci and Piccolomini families. These were the centre tiles of a unit composed of a square tile surrounded by four hexagonal tiles, as seen on the previous pages. Siena, Italy, 1509–13

Overleaf This maiolica tile pavement was commissioned by Bartolomeo Lombardini for the chapel he had built in the now demolished Church of San Francesco Grande in Forlì. It exhibits the fashionable style of the combination of different shapes – trapezoids, diamonds and octagons – to form an overall pattern. Forlì, Italy, c.1513–23

Previous pages This section of magnificent pavement comes from the Château d'Écouen, near Paris, which was built as a hunting lodge by Anne de Montmorency, Constable of France. His celebrated faience tiles were intended to impress his royal guests. Masséot Abaquesne workshop, Rouen, France, *c.*1550

Above and opposite The earliest dateable appearance of glazed tile decoration in the historical region of Bengal on the Indian subcontinent is at the Eklakhi Tomb in Pandua, generally accepted as the mausoleum of Sultan Jalal al-Din Muhammad Shah. By the late 15th century the use of glazed tiles had become more widespread, although confined to Muslim buildings. The glazed architectural tiles on these pages are moulded border tiles, decorated in white on a dark blue ground. From the ruined city of Gaur on the India–Bangladesh border, Bengal, India, late 15th or early 16th century

Above and opposite These two diamond shaped tiles are also from the ruined city of Gaur (see pp.76–7). Terracotta, the natural building material of the region, is well suited to fluent relief decoration as seen in the hand-cut full relief design above.

While traditional Indian ceramics are generally unglazed for practical and religious reasons, new motifs and glazes were introduced from Central Asia and Iran by at least the 13th century. Both the floral designs of these tiles have been painted in enamel colours on a white ground. Bengal, India–Bangladesh border, India, late 15th or early 16th century

Above and opposite These portraits could be idealized images or they could represent two of the Nine Worthies (virtuous historic and fictional characters), a theme which was popular at the time. They are stamped in relief and decorated with coloured lead glazes. Normandy, France, *c.*1500–50

Overleaf Tiles made in the Iberian peninsula
blend techniques and designs from Islamic
and Christian cultures. Here we see the *arista*
technique combined with Renaissance motifs
of Neoclassical forms and grotesque ornament.
Muel, Spain, *c.*1550–1600

Above and opposite Tile-making on a large scale was made possible with the *arista* technique. Designs were impressed into the formed tile with a mould, producing raised ridges. Coloured glazes were applied to different parts of the pattern, the ridges keeping the glazes separate. Toledo, Spain, *c*.1525–50

Opposite and above These *arista* ceiling tile pairs were originally in the Church of Santiago in Carmona, southwest Spain. They were painted in coloured glazes and lustred. Each is moulded with part of a complete floral design, such as quatrefoils containing a rosette or a rayed circle centred on a flower, alternating with shaped panels containing a foliate design. Seville, Spain, 1525–50

Overleaf These two tiles from a set of four were executed in the *cuerda seca* technique in which the design is lightly pressed into the formed tile and the outlines painted in a resist that kept the coloured glazes of the pattern separate. Toledo, Spain, late 15th or early 16th century

Above When northern and central Europe experienced particularly harsh winters in the 16th century, wood-burning stoves became more commonplace, such as this one made for the Convent of St Wolfgang by Hans Kraut. Villingen, Germany, 1577

Opposite Stove tiles were made with moulds so that multiple copies could be produced. Tiles depicting St George (opposite, left) were numerous after the First Crusade. Heraldry was also widespread (opposite, right). These two tiles are covered with a copper-rich green lead glaze. Germany, late 15th or early 16th century

Opposite and above Stove tiles often have imagery that reflects current events and interests. The Council of Trent (1545–63) reaffirmed canonical texts and sacraments of the Church during the religious conflicts in the West. Here we see biblical scenes of the Old Testament's Book of Tobias (opposite) and the New Testament story of the Adoration of the Magi (above, left), and a figure representing Faith (above, right). Germany, mid-16th century

Overleaf A palette of sage green, which has an almost greyish tone, is used here to outline the sprays of tulips and long serrated saz leaves, combined with manganese purple and blue over a white slip. This palette is characteristic of glazed fritware from Damascus and the prevailing stylistic mode of the Ottoman imperial capital at Istanbul. Damascus, Syria, 1550–1600

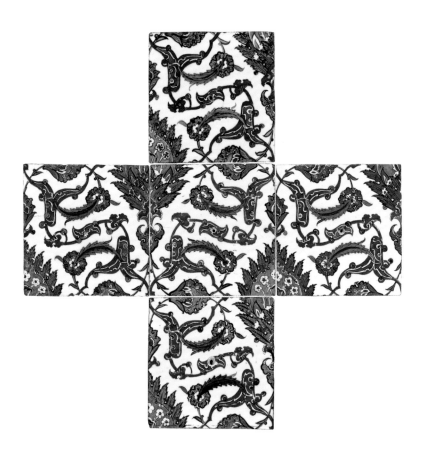

Above Iznik became an established centre of ceramic production in the 15th century, known for its colourful glazed fritware with cobalt-blue decoration. In the 16th century the bright red colour shown in this panel, painted on a bright white slip, was introduced. Iznik, Turkey, *c*.1560–90

Opposite These wall tiles from a lunette-shaped fritware panel probably decorated the imperial palace at Edirne, north-west of Istanbul. The central section of the design is filled with floral and arabesque scrollwork painted in underglaze colours on a white ground. Iznik, Turkey, 1570–4

Previous pages Tiles with this design are associated with the shrine of Eyüp in Istanbul. Each group of four fritware tiles has the complete pattern, which is symmetrical on the vertical axis, allowing it to be repeated endlessly, like a textile design. Placing a tulip inside each of the large turquoise serrated saz leaves is a stylistic innovation of the late 1570s. Iznik, Turkey, *c.*1580

Above This spandrel-shaped fritware tile panel was probably made to fit over the large windows of a mosque prayer hall. A cloud band in red intertwines with scrollwork set with green leaves and blue rosettes, painted in underglaze on white in this self-contained design. Iznik, Turkey, 1570–5

Opposite These six glazed fritware tiles show the partial repetition of a complex painted pattern. They combine an oversized arabesque in red with fantastic blossoms formed from smaller flowers and leaves. One motif is superimposed on another, but there is no attempt to create an illusion of depth. Instead, the motifs are laid out over the flat surface of the tile. Iznik, Turkey, 1570–80

Opposite and above These five hexagonal fritware tiles are painted in blue and turquoise on white slip with stylized floral designs. The motifs include a cloud-pattern, lotus flower, prunus tree and a pair of ducks amid scrolling stems, showing the influence of blue-and-white Chinese ceramics. Iznik, Turkey, 1540–50

Overleaf This abstract panel of hexagonal fritware tiles has turquoise glazing and patterning in black. The pairs of wavy lines and groups of three large dots may represent tiger stripes and leopard spots, or Chinese cloud bands. Turkey or Syria, 1550–1600

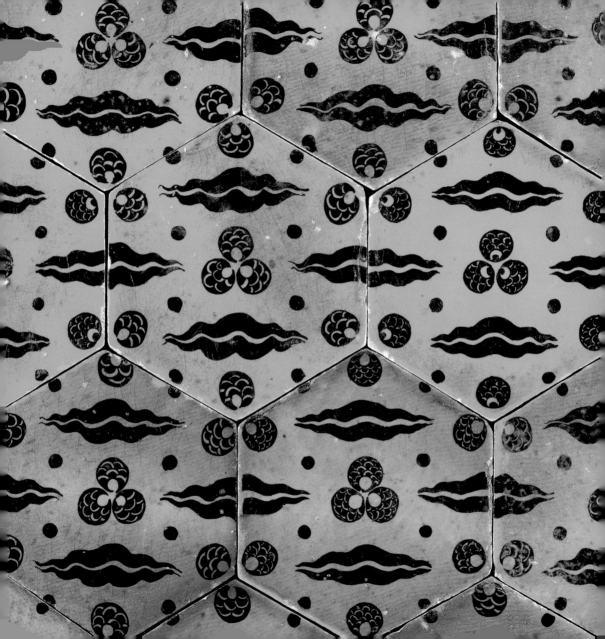

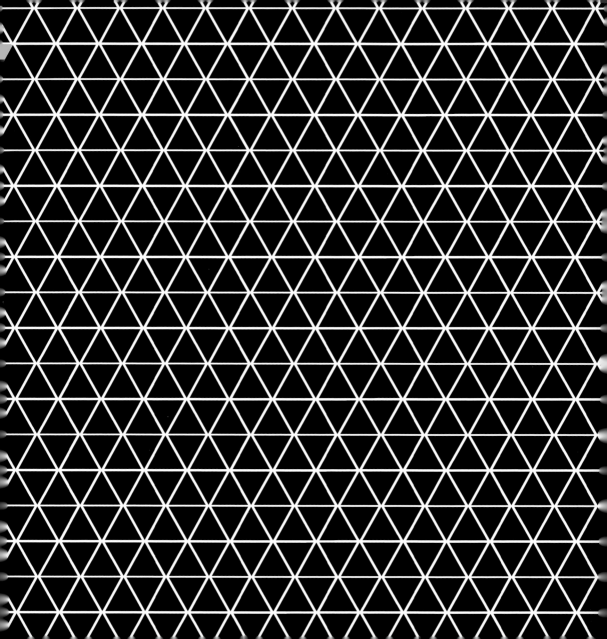

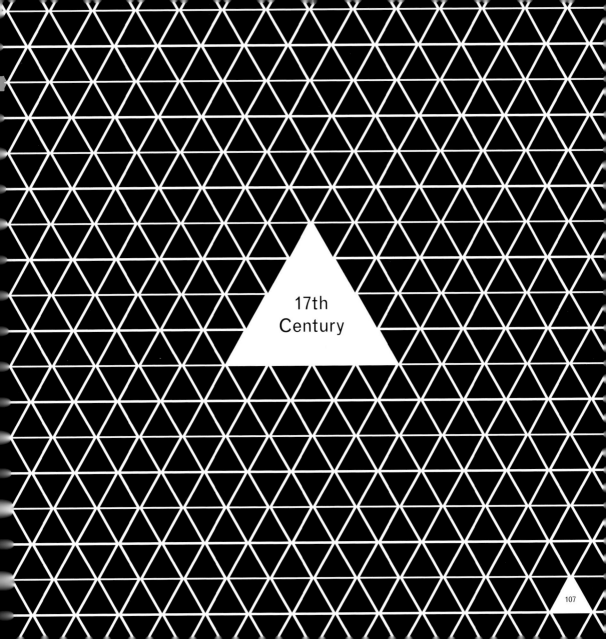

17th
Century

Previous pages, opposite and above
These fritware tile panels are filled
with flowers: tulips, irises, carnations,
hyacinths and roses covering the
background or springing from tankards
and vases are interspersed with cyprus
and prunus trees. These are painted freely
in cobalt blue, olive green, turquoise
and manganese-purple underglaze over
a white slip. Figurative designs are
unusual in Syrian tiles; two birds drinking
from a fountain (opposite) is a common
Byzantine motif. Damascus, Syria,
late 16th or early 17th century

Overleaf The bold, geometric, repeat
floral pattern of this tile panel displays
the distinctive Syrian colour palette of
blue, green, turquoise and purple over a
white slip. Damascus, Syria, late 16th or
early 17th century

Above and opposite These two tiles were probably made for a bathhouse or palace. Depicting two female figures with henna-stained hands on a background of flowers and birds, these examples of Iranian Kubachi ware reflect the influence of Iznik imports, using a similar red colour in the painted polychrome underglaze. Probably Isfahan, Iran, 1600–25

Overleaf Often found in palaces in Iran, large-scale tile panels with figural decoration contrast to the resolutely non-figural tilework made in contemporary Ottoman Turkey. Painted in colours on white slip and outlined in black in the *cuerda seca* technique, springtime scenes of outdoor meals or entertainment were popular in the art and poetry of the time. Isfahan, Iran, 17th century

Previous pages, opposite, above and overleaf In the early decades of the 17th century a new type of tilework spread across historic Panjab, in the northern provinces of the Mughal empire, likely to have been derived from Iran and used on monuments associated with Iranian patrons. It was used on some important monuments associated with noble tombs, such as the tomb of Asaf Khan in Lahore (previous pages and opposite) and the tomb and mosque of Sayyid Muhammad al-Madini in Kashmir. The tiles were made using the *cuerda seca* technique and painted in bright colours with stylized and naturalistic foliate designs. (Previous pages and opposite) Lahore, Pakistan, mid-17th century; (above and overleaf) Kashmir, India, mid-17th century

124

Opposite, above and overleaf These delftware tiles reflect the varied interests and multicultural heritage of the Dutch peoples. Printed books illustrating vegetation provided tile painters with inspiration, as shown by the pomegranates, grapes and tulips here. The Iberian geometrical designs forming multipart patterns overleaf are inherited from their Spanish–Hapsburg rulers. Netherlands, late 16th or early 17th century

Above Animals were often depicted on delftware tiles, including many species from far away countries, copied from illustrated printed books. Netherlands, late 16th or early 17th century

Opposite The Dutch also had a particular fascination for tulips, selling bulbs at extraordinarily high prices until the market collapsed in 1637. Netherlands, late 16th or early 17th century

Above and opposite This wood-burning tile stove is composed of faience panels depicting contemporary cultural and religious interests. Scenes of Roman history and mythology, allegorical virtues and vices are intermingled with moralizing tiles such as the one above advising people to modify their behaviour because the world is watching. (Above) Switzerland, early 17th century; (opposite) Winterthur, Switzerland, late 17th century

The Plot first hatcht at Rome
by the Pope and Cardinalls
&c.

The Conspirators Signeing y.e Resolue
for killing the King.

Father Connyers Preaching against y.e
Oathes of Alejance & Supremacy.

D.r Oates discovereth y.e Plot. to
y.e King and Councell.

C.t bedlow discoverer
of the plott.

Cap.t bedlow examind by y.e secret
Comitee of the house of
Commons.

Pickerin attempts to kill y.e K.
in S.t Iames Park.

Pickerin Executed.

S.r William waller burning Popish
books Images and Relatues.

Opposite Scandal was as popular in the 17th century as it is today. Like a modern tabloid newspaper, the delftware tile panel here depicts scenes from the fabricated Popish Plot (1678–81). It was painted with cobalt blue on a white tin glaze by Dutch craftsmen working in England. England, *c.*1680

Above This tile, depicting King Charles II, the intended victim of the Popish Plot, was made in the Netherlands for the English market. Netherlands, 1660–75

Opposite and this page Purple, made from manganese, was another popular colour used to paint delftware tiles in both England and the Netherlands. Depictions of mounted and foot soldiers are often found on Dutch tiles, reflecting the historic conflict between the northern Dutch Republic and the southern Spanish-held provinces. Probably Harlingen, Netherlands, late 17th century

Whaling was a popular subject for the seafaring
Dutch. This delftware tile panel, painted in
cobalt blue, is signed by the painter Cornelis
Bouwmeester, who specialized in painting
large scenes on multi-tile panels. Rotterdam,
Netherlands, *c*.1700

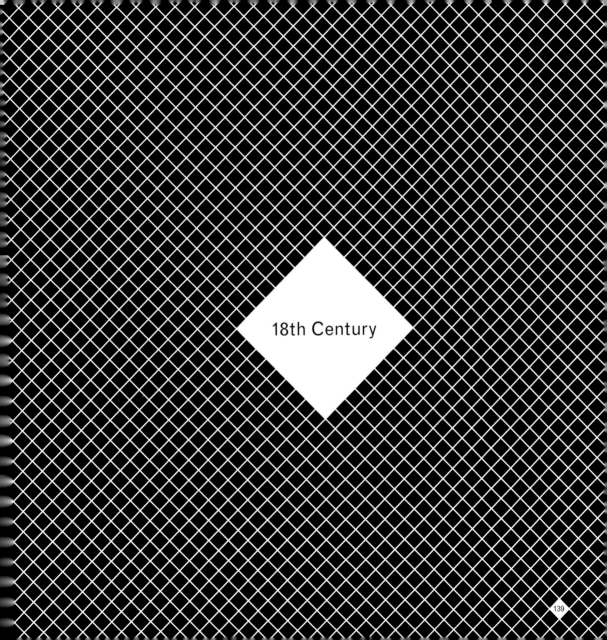

18th Century

Previous pages The Portuguese court was noted for its love of pleasure and cultural pursuits. In this finely painted multipart tile panel from the Music Room of the Quinta Formosa, we see members of the aristocracy engaging in reading, music-playing and dancing, all in a sumptuous garden setting. Lisbon, Portugal, c.1720–30

Opposite and above Not every region in Europe banned the use of images or tolerated only biblical scenes from the Old Testament during the religious wars of the 16th and 17th centuries. Here we see manganese-purple painted tiles depicting religious scenes from both the Old and the New Testaments. Netherlands, 18th century

Opposite and above Waterside images were very popular in the Netherlands and were often copied by tile painters in England. Here we see scenes of fishing and windmills, both important aspects of the Dutch economy. These elaborate cobalt-painted tiles were costly to produce and were probably made for wealthy merchants. (Opposite) Netherlands, 18th century; (above) Liverpool, England, 1750–5

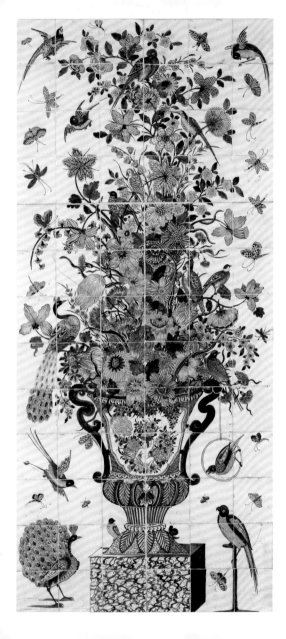

Left and opposite Tile painters would have needed to use patterns to compose a multi-tile panel such as this one depicting an elaborate flower vase dotted with birds. The cost of this complicated tilework explains why such panels are found primarily in aristocratic residences. Similar ones were made for the Château de Rambouillet, near Paris, and the Amalienburg Pavilion of Schloss Nymphenburg, near Munich. Delft, Netherlands, *c.*1710–50

These charming tiles were painted in many colours in maiolica workshops in the Catalonia region of Spain, which specialized in *rajoles de oficis* (tiles depicting trades). They were retrieved from a house in Palma on the island of Mallorca before its demolition. Spain, late 18th or early 19th century

Opposite and above As early as the 1560s, Dutch delftware makers of Italian descent took the technique of painted tin-glazed earthenware to England. Consequently, much English delftware has similarities to that of the Netherlands. Here we see tiles painted with Chinese figures, reflecting knowledge of the East gained through trade by both the Dutch and English East Indies Companies. Liverpool, England, c.1750–5

MR WROUGHTON

in the Character of BARNWELL

Above and opposite John Sadler and Guy Green perfected
the technique of transfer printing onto tin-glazed tiles.
This was dramatically cheaper than hand-painting which
previously dominated the market. These tiles, probably
made for a fireplace, depict two popular actors of the
English stage, revealing a widespread passion for
the theatre. Liverpool, England, *c.*1777–80

Mrs LESSINGHAM

in the Character of OPHELIA

Above and opposite Transfer-printed tiles dominated
the English tile market in the later 18th century. Here we
see scenes of idealized bucolic life in an age when small
landholdings were being merged into larger farms on
a massive scale. Trajan's Column in Rome (above, left)
was one of the must-sees amongst the upper classes who
went on the Grand Tour of the classical world. Liverpool,
England, c.1758–61

Above, opposite and overleaf Imitating other materials
in the arts has a long history. Here we see tiles with
patterns applied with coloured slips (watered-down clay)
and paint to imitate marble. They may have been placed
on the lower parts of walls as an elaborate marble-like
wainscoting in tilework. Either plain tiles or a plastered
surface would have been used on the walling above them.
(Above and opposite) England, 18th century; (overleaf)
Netherlands, 18th century

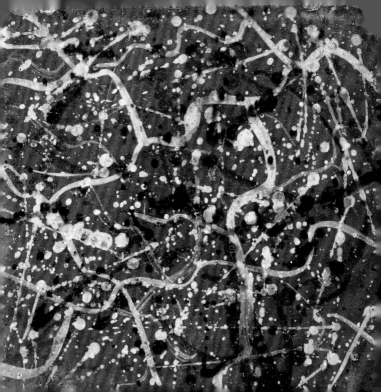

Opposite This terracotta relief panel would originally have been made for the exterior of a Hindu temple in Bengal and depicts a scene from the great Hindu epic *The Ramayana*, which tells the story of Rama, an incarnation of the god Vishnu. India, 17th or 18th century

Above These two sections of friezes are from the brick temple of Gopinath in Jashore (Jessore) District, Bangladesh. The top panel shows a cow and calf from the herds guarded by Krishna in childhood. Krishna himself is shown ripping open the beak of the crane-demon Bakasura, sent to kill him by the tyrant king Kansa (top). The frieze below shows Krishna followed by a procession of cowherds blowing horns. Bangladesh, *c*.1749

The designs of this individual fritware tile from a
decorated chimney piece belong mostly to the repertory
of ornament developed by the Ottoman court in the
16th century, such as the 'tiger-stripe and leopard-spot'
motif shown on this tile. It is painted in with polychrome
underglaze. After a decline in Iznik tiles during the
17th century, a revival supported by the Ottoman court
relocated the tile industry to Istanbul in the early 18th
century. Istanbul, Turkey, c.1731

The main motif painted on this fritware tile is a calligraphic pattern formed from the names of God, the prophet Muhammad and the first four caliphs – Abu Bakr, 'Umar, 'Uthman and 'Ali – marking the Ottoman dynasty's adherence to Sunni Islam. Istanbul, Turkey, c.1727

19th Century

Previous pages The Gothic Revival building boom of the 19th century led to many commissions for flooring in churches and other public buildings. These two floor-tile sections contain heraldic charges of fleurs-de-lys and addorsed (back-to-back) birds that are used solely as design elements. William Godwin & Son, Herefordshire, England, *c.*1865

Above An inlaid tile from Salisbury Cathedral in Wiltshire that dates from the restorations of the English architect George Gilbert Scott in the 1860s. The heraldic design of addorsed birds was copied from surviving examples from the late 13th-century flooring at Salisbury Cathedral itself. William Godwin & Son, Herefordshire, England, 1863–70

Opposite Walter Chamberlain, along with Herbert Minton, bought into Samuel Wright's 1828 patent for the manufacture of inlaid tiles. The original for this pattern was in the 15th-century flooring of a church in Marlborough, Wiltshire. Commissioners of such tiles were usually the architects responsible for the building projects. Worcester, England, *c.*1840

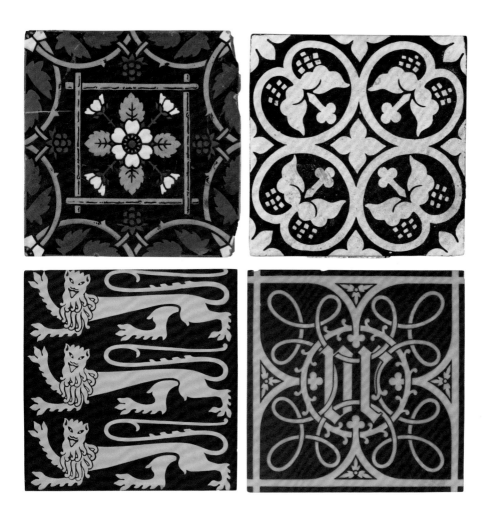

Above and opposite Designers, architects and tile manufacturers were inspired by the patterns on medieval inlaid tiles; they either copied them exactly or made variations. The tiles on these pages were made by Minton & Co., Stoke-on-Trent, Maw & Co., Broseley, and Robert Minton Taylor, Fenton, England, c.1848–80.

A.W.N. Pugin, the English designer–architect, produced many medieval-style designs while working with Minton & Co., some of which were made for the Palace of Westminster in London, England. Stoke-on-Trent, England, 19th century

Above These tiles from Alton Towers in Staffordshire were designed by A.W.N. Pugin for the Earl of Shrewsbury and made by Minton & Co., which published the designs in *Examples of Old English Tiles* (1842), the first printed catalogue illustrating 'appropriate' designs for medieval restoration. Stoke-on-Trent, England, 1842–4

Opposite At the centre of these tiles from the sanctuary of St George's Roman Catholic Cathedral in Southwark, London, is the Agnus Dei ('Lamb of God'), a symbol of Jesus Christ. This design was created by A.W.N. Pugin and was used in other commissions as well, such as for the Church of St Giles in Cheadle, Staffordshire. Minton & Co., Stoke-on-Trent, England, *c*.1850

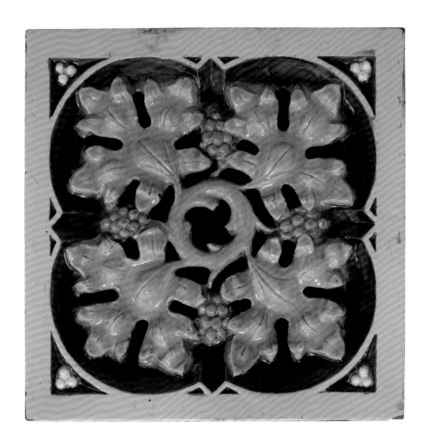

Above and opposite These two tiles come from a stove designed by A.W.N. Pugin for the Medieval Court at London's Great Exhibition of 1851 where he launched his majolica-glazed tiles, developed by the French ceramicist Léon Arnoux at Minton & Co. in the late 1840s. Such durable majolica tiles were suitable for heavy use and, combined with high-relief decoration, were attractive accompaniments to architectural interiors. Minton & Co. went on to produce such tiles for the Royal Dairy at Windsor and for the original buildings of the Victoria and Albert Museum (then known as the South Kensington Museum). Stoke-on-Trent, England, *c.*1850

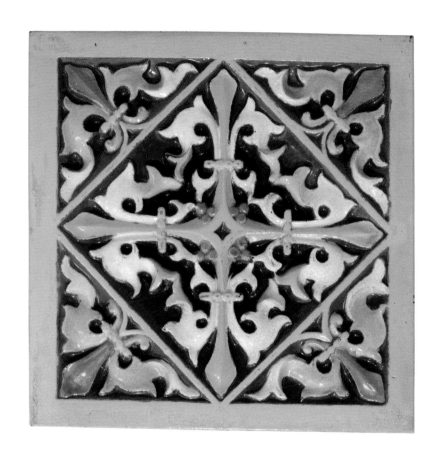

Previous pages, above and opposite While Minton
attracted most of the attention at London's Great
Exhibition in 1851 and was a major producer during
the Gothic Revival period, the competition was to
become fierce during the second half of the 19th century.
Technological advances in tile-making and decorating
meant that quality tiles could be produced quickly,
consistently and affordably, rapidly expanding the
industry. By the mid-1860s tiles were a typical feature
in the middle-class home in Britain and continued in
popularity through the Edwardian period (1901–10).
The tiles on these pages were produced by a range of
British manufacturers. Britain, mid- to late 19th century

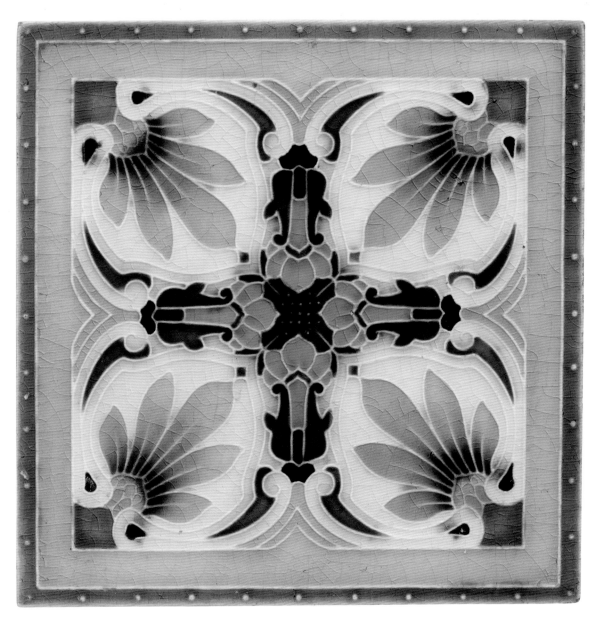

Opposite and above In the latter part of the 19th century in Britain, a vast array of wall and fireplace tiles appeared on the market alongside the well-established range of floor tiles. Indoor bathrooms became commonplace following the arrival of running water in the 1870s and these rooms were covered in decorative tilework.

The relief patterns of these earthenware wall tiles are forerunners of the Art Nouveau style with their moulded foliate patterns. (Opposite) Minton's China Works, Fenton, England, *c.*1890; (above) Maw & Co., Bromley, Shropshire, England, *c.*1885

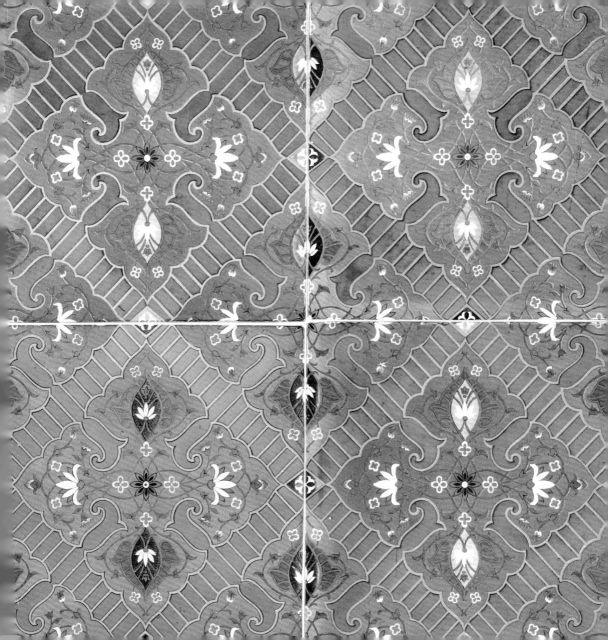

Previous pages, above and opposite Following the success of the Great Exhibition in London in 1851, other nations also put on exhibitions to promote design and manufactures. These tiles were purchased at the 1867 Exposition Universelle in Paris. They were probably made by the L.A.C. Macé porcelain factory in Paris, which exhibited its newly patented process of chromolithographic transfer printing onto ceramics at the fair. Paris, France, 19th century

Overleaf In spite of the popularity of the Gothic Revival movement in Europe in the first half of the 19th century, not all designers and manufacturers concentrated solely on the medieval style. This blue-glazed relief tile panel, perhaps originally inset in a piece of furniture, bears images of cupids and acanthus flowers that are closer to the Neoclassical taste for the art of Ancient Greece and Rome. France, c.1845

Opposite and above Produced by the Sèvres porcelain factory, this panel of four tiles was exhibited in the Exposition Universelle in Paris in 1867. The panel's geometric design takes inspiration from Spanish and Islamic tilework and was executed in the *arista* technique. Sèvres, France, *c.*1867

Right In Spain and Portugal, where the production of handmade tin-glazed tiles had continued in an unbroken tradition, the adoption of new production techniques was more gradual.

Spanish tile-making was represented in the Great Exhibition of 1851 by the Valencian factory of Rafael Gonzalez Valls, including this panel of hexagonal tiles with painted decoration using a stencil on mass-produced solid clay tiles. Valencia, Spain, *c.*1850

Previous pages, opposite, above and overleaf Although
continuing in the tin-glazed tradition, the firm of Rafael
Gonzalez Valls pioneered the use of stencilling alongside
more traditional hand-painting on a tin-glazed surface.
The stencilled designs show the growing stylistic
eclecticism of the century, when geometric patterns
associated with Spain's Islamic past were given
contemporary treatments, while others reflect
the lingering Neoclassicism typical of the tilework
of Valencia and Onda. Valencia, Spain, *c.*1850

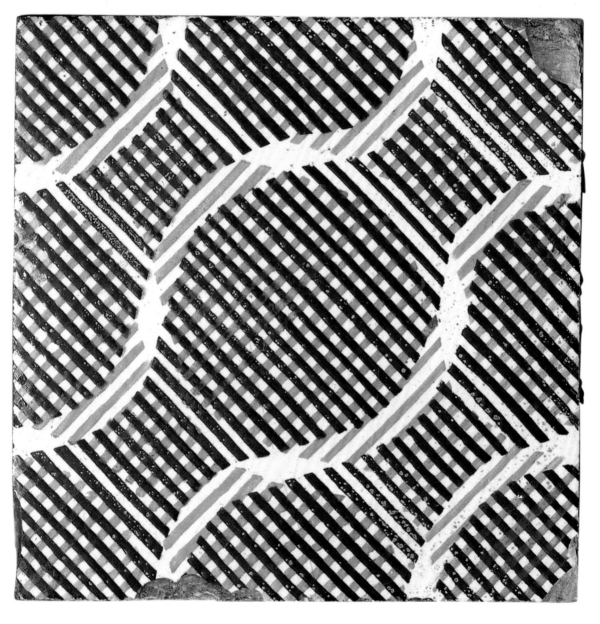

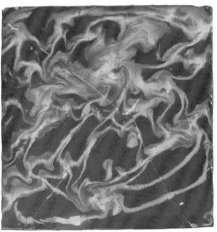

Above and opposite The Rafael Gonzalez Valls tile manufactory also experimented with coloured glazes to produce brightly coloured tiles with a marbleized appearance. These were also exhibited at the Great Exhibition in London, England, 1851. Valencia, Spain, *c.*1850

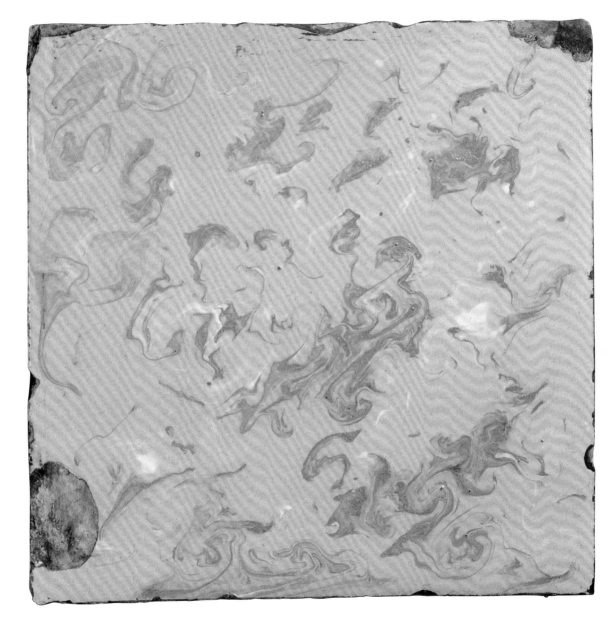

Opposite and above As a reaction to the seemingly unstoppable process of industrialization, hand-painted tiles became a popular feature of artistic interiors, especially in the 1860s and 1870s. William Morris, who founded the furnishings and decorative arts firm Morris, Marshall, Faulkner & Co. in London in 1861, hand-painted designs onto white, tin-glazed blanks, often imported from the Netherlands.

Designed by William Morris, the 'Tulip and Trellis' tile (opposite) was painted by Morris's associate William De Morgan, while the tile above was designed by Philip Webb for Morris & Co. London, England, both *c.*1870

Opposite and right Decorated with motifs of scrolling acanthus leaves and daisies, these tiles were designed by William Morris for a bathroom in Membland Hall, near Plymouth, Devon. Probably due to his lack of experience in scaling up a design over numerous tiles, Morris asked William De Morgan to draw up the complicated multi-tile pattern and execute the paintwork.

The design remained on Morris & Co.'s stocklists until 1912–13 and a number of panels, other than the six made for Membland, are known to exist. London, England, *c.*1876

This page and opposite Although not a great commercial success, William De Morgan became the leading pottery and tile manufacturer associated with the Arts and Crafts and Aesthetic movements. The two hand-painted tiles on this page have been painted onto dust-pressed blanks, featuring the 'Oblique Leaf' design in green and 'Flying Leaf' design in manganese, both with the rose mark of De Morgan's London workshop, Sand's End Pottery in Fulham, which opened in 1888.

The tile opposite, decorated with stylized carnations and foliage, was produced at his earlier Merton Abbey workshop in London, where Morris & Co. also operated from the early 1880s. England, *c.*1880s

This pattern, with flower heads facing in alternating directions, was probably the most popular of all of De Morgan's tile designs. It was known as 'BBB', after the Norwich firm of Barnard, Bishop and Barnard who made cast-iron fireplaces and supplied De Morgan tiles to use with them. These four earthenware tiles, hand-painted on a white tin-glazed surface, were made by his firm, Sand's End Pottery, London, England, 1898

This page De Morgan did not only hand-paint tiles but his technique for transferring patterns to tiles was unusual. Rather than pouncing the design, the decoration was painted onto a sheet of fine tissue placed on a sheet of glass, behind which an outline of the pattern acted as a guide. The tissue was then placed face-down on the slip-coated surface of the tile and covered with a clear glaze. During the firing the tissue would burn away. London, England, 1870s–80s

This page and overleaf De Morgan accidentally set fire to his parents' house in 1871 while trying to produce lustreware in a kiln in the cellar. Establishing himself at Cheyne Row in Chelsea, London, the following year, he perfected the lustre technique and developed a particularly rich 'ruby' lustre (overleaf). He also developed a range of 'Persian' colours (primarily blue, turquoise and green), which were close to the palette of earlier Syrian tiles. London, England, 1870s

Above William De Morgan also experimented with different reactive coloured glazes at his Sand's End Pottery in Fulham, London. These tiles would have been used either on their own or placed as borders around the more decorative tiles he painted and lustred. London, England, late 19th century

Opposite Maw & Co. had an ongoing relationship with the Museum of Practical Geology in London, contributing to research in relation to British clays, and in 1881 Maw & Co. requested casts of fossils to use in decorating tiles. These tiles, including an impressed trilobite design, reflect both a trend for stylized natural designs identified with Art Nouveau and a much earlier tradition of creating designs cast from natural objects, as seen in the work of Renaissance potter Bernard Palissy. Jackfield, Shropshire, England, *c.*1860–80

Overleaf Maw & Co. also worked with prominent designers, such as Walter Crane and Lewis Day, to create more costly hand-painted work not intended for the mass market. 'Ploughing' by Crane formed the lower frieze of a large tile panel on the theme of labour designed by both Crane and Day. Ironbridge, Shropshire, England, *c.*1889

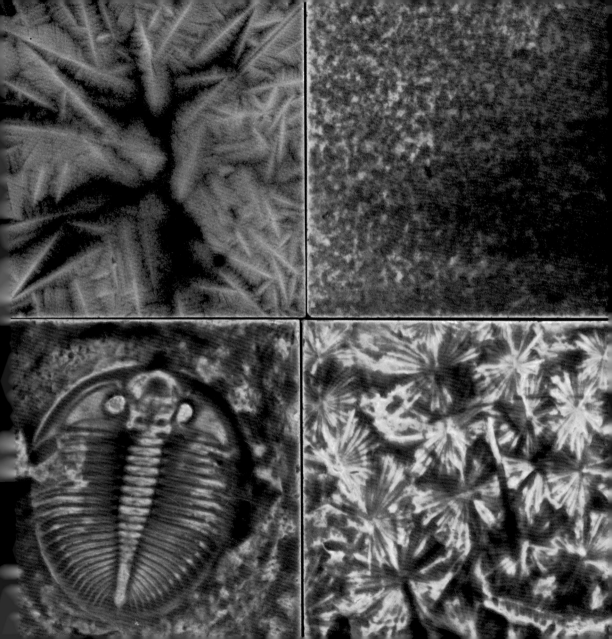

AVTVMN

WINTER

SPRING

SVMMER

Previous pages, opposite and right The South Kensington Museum (now the Victoria and Albert Museum) opened its Refreshment Rooms in 1868, the world's first museum dining facilities. The artist Edward J. Poynter was commissioned to design the Dutch Kitchen or Grill Room, now known as the Poynter Room.

On the upper walls, sets of painted tiles represent the months and seasons, as well as the signs of the zodiac. Below, fruit and flowers are interspersed among portraits of women from classical literature, including Helen, Venus, Medea and Sappho. The tiles were painted by female students attending a special porcelain class for ladies at the National Art Training School in London, an unusual public commission for women at this time. London, England, late 1860s

Above In the later 19th century, Qajar artists began to imitate the art of the Safavid period, copying the colourful, monumental 17th-century tile panels that decorated palaces in Isfahan (see pp.116–17). This painted fritware tile was commissioned by the French composer Alfred Lemaire from ceramic artist 'Ali Muhammad Isfahani. Tehran, Iran, 1884–5

Opposite This moulded design of a falconer on horseback painted in turquoise, pink and yellow with black outline, against a stylized floral background on a blue ground, was an extremely popular European import with multiple similar tiles found in the Victoria and Albert Museum's collection. Isfahan, Iran, 1850–65

Opposite The garden scene depicting a man and woman against an architectural background echoes the Armenian architecture of Isfahan. The moulded glazed fritware is painted in underglaze pigments including blue, turquoise, pink, yellow and black. Isfahan, Iran, 1865–85

Above This large tile depicts the famous scene of the Sasanian king Khosrow coming across the Armenian princess Shirin bathing, from the 12th-century Iranian poem *Khamsa* (*Five Tales*) by Nizami Ganjavi. In the mid-19th century, tiles like these were sold as individual objects for display, rather than as multipart friezes, and many were acquired by western tourists and visitors as souvenirs. Isfahan, Iran, 1880–5

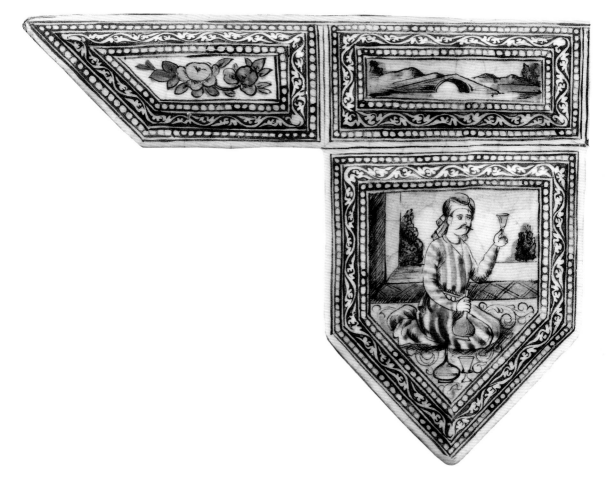

Opposite and above The painting style of this interlocking fritware tile panel, made by 'Ali Muhammad Isfahani, shows the strong influence of European art. The central scene depicts royalty from pre-Islamic Iran, a popular period of history at this time, with individual figures reading, riding or pouring wine at each point of the star. Tehran, Iran, 1887

Overleaf This panel of 96 glazed tiles with *cuerda seca* decoration depicting birds and flowering stems against a yellow ground comes from the demolished south gate of the Top-Maidan (Artillery Square) in Tehran. The South Kensington Museum (now the Victoria and Albert Museum) bought this tile panel in late 1876, in a set of six very similar panels; the square had just been extended and redeveloped, and the tile panels came from the recently demolished perimeter. Tehran, Iran, 1800–25

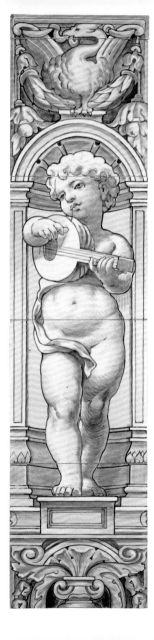

Left and opposite These tiles were part of a wider decorative scheme for the Criterion, a 'gastronomic temple' with dining rooms, grand hall and theatre at Piccadilly Circus, London. The Criterion was designed by Thomas Verity and completed in 1873.

The tiles were designed and painted by A.S. Coke for W.B. Simpson & Sons. This section of the tile scheme was probably designed for the buffet area and was rediscovered when the building was renovated in 1969. The tiles were made in Staffordshire and painted in London. Stoke-on-Trent and London, England, *c.*1872

Opposite and right Minton's China Works was founded by Colin Minton Campbell following his spilt with Michael Dainty Hollins, with whom he had run the Minton firm since Herbert Minton's death in 1858. Hollins retained the tile business and name, Minton, Hollins & Co. and Minton & Co. With the benefits of art education and training in mind, Campbell also founded Minton's Art Pottery Studio in South Kensington, London, in 1871.

A variety of notable British designers and illustrators, including Henry Stacy Marks, William Wise and John Moyr Smith, became associated with Minton's during this period. These block-printed tiles were designed by Moyr Smith and depict scenes from William Shakespeare's plays. Stoke-on-Trent, England, *c.*1873

Above and opposite Pictorial tile series like these were often part of a 19th-century British fireplace which, to improve efficiency in the home, had a vertical opening with a canopy hood and splayed tiled cheeks. The design of the grate made tiles an obligatory feature, though one that could be mixed and matched according to taste.

These tiles are from series pattern No. 1347, 'Spirit of the Flowers', possibly designed by C.O. Murray for Minton & Co. The complete set of 12 included 'waterlily, wild rose, poppy, lily of the valley, daisy, foxglove, violet, convolvulus, anemone, snowdrop, lily and primrose'. Stoke-on-Trent, England, *c.*1880

233

Above and opposite The English artist and book illustrator Walter Crane designed these tiles for Maw & Co. They depict the classical figures of Zephyria, holding a globe in one hand and a fan in the other, and Ignis, who flies through the air while holding a thunderbolt in each hand. They were part of a set of tiles produced for the firm on the theme of the 'Four Elements'. Jackfield, Shropshire, England, late 19th century

Above and opposite These animated tiles are from a series decorated with scenes from Aesop's *Fables*, including 'The Crow and the Wine Jar' and 'The Fox and the Grapes' shown here, which was produced by Minton, Hollins & Co. The designs were possibly painted by Clement Heaton, founder of the stained-glass firm Heaton, Butler and Bayne, whose work can be seen in, amongst other places, Westminster Abbey in London and Peterborough Cathedral in Cambridgeshire, England. Made in Stoke-on-Trent, England, *c.*1875

Above and opposite Block-printed with hand-coloured decoration, these tiles, depicting humorous scenes of children performing daily domestic tasks, were designed by the artist and children's book illustrator Elizabeth Ellen Houghton for Minton's China Works. In their form, they resemble the medieval Labours of the Months in which certain tasks, appropriate to a particular month, are portrayed in a variety of mediums, including painted ones. Made in Stoke-on-Trent, England, *c*.1880

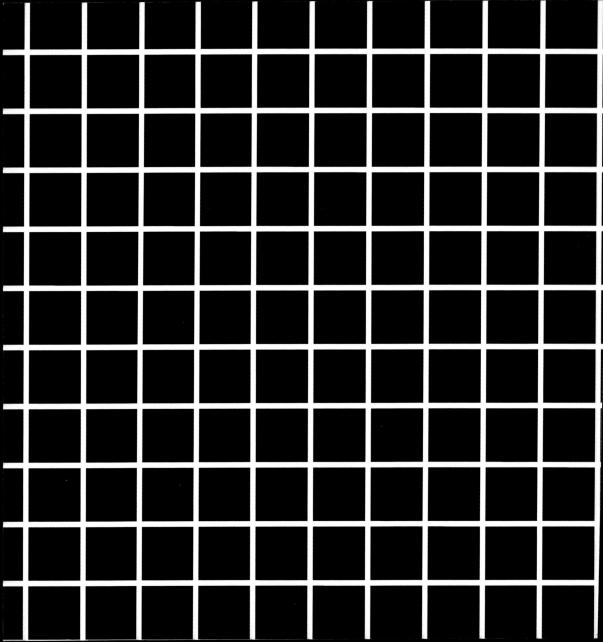

20th to 21st Century

Opposite and above The artist Walter Crane designed these tiles, entitled 'Flora's Train', for Pilkington's Tile and Pottery Company, Clifton Junction, Manchester, England. As in some of his own book illustrations, Crane has here epitomized the freedom of line so characteristic of the Art Nouveau style. In order to make multiple copies of the tiles, Pilkington's employed moulds rather than trailing slip lines by hand (tube-lining) to create the raised line patterns. Manchester, England, 1900–1

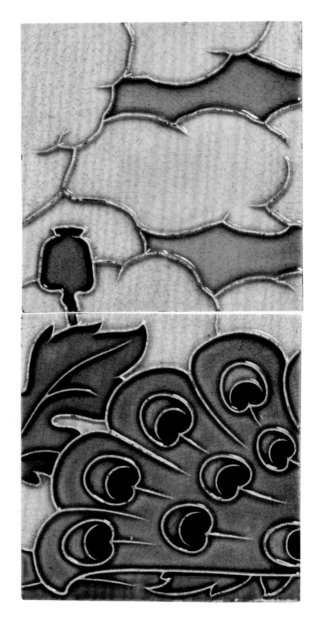

In this stunning panel, the tile decorator employed
tube-lining, a free-hand method of drawing a design
with raised lines made of slip. The various coloured
glazes would be contained within the raised lines and not
blend into one another. Peacocks were a popular motif
in the Art Nouveau period because of the multicoloured
patterns in their tails. Possibly made by Pilkington's Tile
and Pottery Company, Manchester, England, c.1900

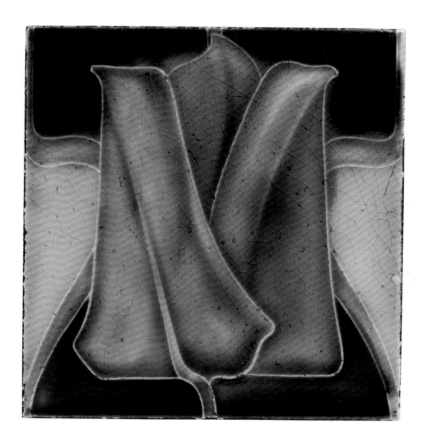

Above This tulip-pattern tile was designed by C.F.A. Voysey for Pilkington's. His innovative designs generally feature motifs from nature that have been distilled to pure flat forms. This tile was made with a mould to produce multiple copies for a wider commercial market. Manchester, England, *c*.1900

Opposite By the same artist, this tile panel features a bird motif, characteristic of Voysey's designs, perched here in a cherry tree. The pattern here was tube-lined by hand. Probably Pilkington's Tile and Pottery Company, Manchester, England, *c*.1903–4

Above and opposite These distinctive green tiles moulded in relief with dolphins, flowers and scrolling foliage were designed for Sainsbury's stores by Minton, Hollins & Co. in about 1900 and were displayed in the counter areas in a frieze just below the ceiling. They were reproduced for many years and became a recognizable motif for the grocers. Stoke-on-Trent, England, *c.*1900

Above This tile was designed and painted by a pupil of the influential art teacher Marion Richardson who developed teaching methods that encouraged self-expression and experimentation rather than traditional copying. English artist Roger Fry, founder of the Omega Workshops, brought Richardson to critical attention in an exhibition of her pupils' work. Possibly Birmingham, England, early 20th century

Opposite This inlaid floor tile was designed by architect and industrial designer Peter Behrens for the German firm Villeroy & Boch. Produced following Behrens's appointment as director of the *Kunstgewerbeschule* (applied art school) in Düsseldorf in 1903, such tiles represent a move away from Art Nouveau to a new design language of geometric and abstract forms. Mettlach, Germany, *c.*1903

Opposite and above These panels of tin-glazed tiles depicting bathers (opposite) and the writer Lytton Strachey (above) were painted by Vanessa Bell and Duncan Grant, respectively. Along with Roger Fry, they were founders of the Omega Workshops, which brought colour, spontaneity and the sensibilities of continental modern art to English interior design.

Bell and Grant continued producing decorative domestic items after the demise of Omega in 1919. Their tiles, which provided an ideal surface for their bold and lively painting styles, were produced at a pottery in south London and sold individually or mounted in wooden frames for trays or tables. London, England, 1926

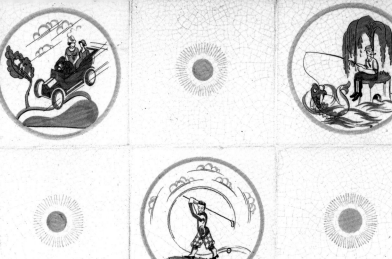

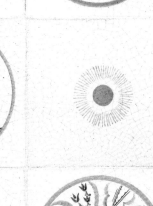

Opposite and above The 'Sporting' series of hand-painted tin-glazed tiles was designed by the artist Edward Bawden for Carter & Co. in the early 1920s, offering a playful and affectionate portrayal of British life typical of his work at the time. Carter's was by this time one of Britain's leading producers of tiles and architectural ceramics. Made in Poole, Dorset, England, *c.*1922

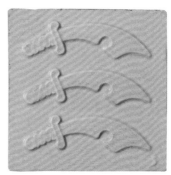

Above and opposite Artist and designer Harold
Stabler designed this series of moulded relief tiles
for use in London Underground stations. The tiles were
commissioned from Carter & Co. by the British Transport
administrator Frank Pick who steered the development of
the London Underground corporate identity and branding.
Many of these tiles are still *in situ* in Bethnal Green
underground station. Poole, Dorset, England, *c.*1939

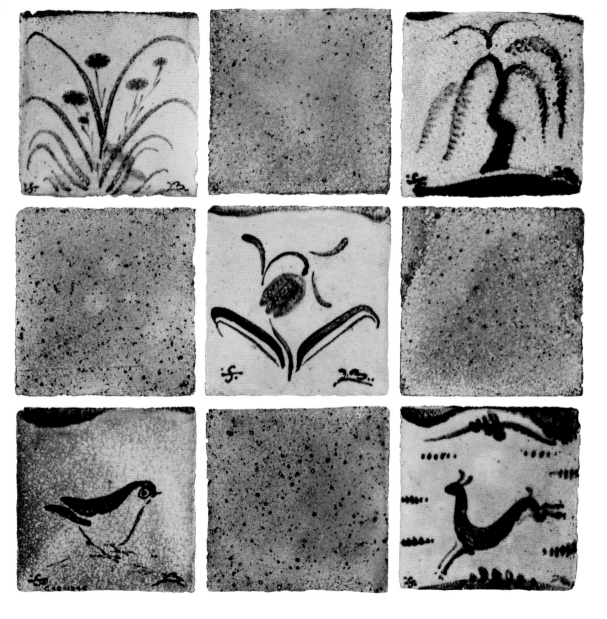

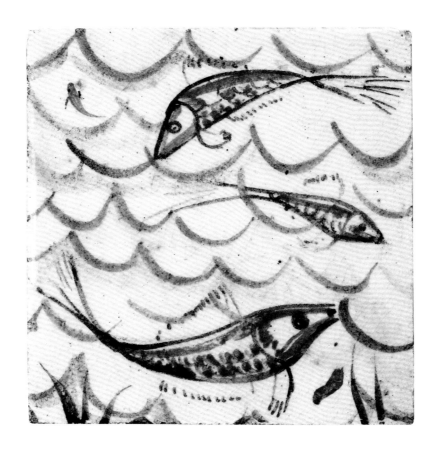

Opposite The pioneer studio potter Bernard Leach began production of handmade and decorated stoneware tiles at St Ives in Cornwall around 1927. They provided the perfect vehicle for Leach's fluid brushwork, the designs exhibiting both English medieval and Japanese influences. St Ives, Cornwall, England, *c.*1939

Above This central tile from a panel of hand-painted tiles depicts a stylized fish pond designed by the English potter Heber Mathews. Like Leach, he was influenced by the 'rustic' aesthetic of early English pottery and the refined simplicity of East Asian traditions. London, England, *c.*1950

Above and opposite In the late 1940s Carter & Co. was experimenting with silkscreen printing onto their plain tiles to create decorative and affordable mass-produced tiles for the building boom after the Second World War. Through her connections with architects, the artist and influential art teacher Peggy Angus began a partnership with Carter's.

Angus's designs, inspired by European and Indonesian folk art, were ideally suited to the post-war Modernist movement, using brightly coloured repeatable patterns to cover large wall surfaces. Carter & Co., Poole, Dorset, England, late 1940s–early 1950s

Above and opposite After training at the Royal College of Art, London, Peggy Angus became an influential art teacher, teaching her students about design and pattern from the Middle Ages to the present. She taught her students to make potato-cut prints, turning the successful ones into linocuts from which they would hand-print wallpapers for the school walls.

These two tiles bear designs originally produced as potato-cut prints and then silkscreened at Carter & Co. Poole, Dorset, England, *c.*1950–5

Above and opposite These three tiles were designed by the artist Laurence Scarfe for the Kenneth Clark Pottery, founded by Kenneth Clark and his wife, Ann Wynn Reeves, and have been screenprinted in gold lustre paste onto commercially manufactured white-glazed tiles.

Through such collaborations, the Clarks promoted the continued production of original and experimental tile decoration by independent artists and workshops. London, England, *c.*1965

Opposite and above Designed by Ann Wynn Reeves, craft-potter tiles like these bring the individuality of artistic design and craft skill to mass-produced tiles. These designs were executed on blanks made by the tile manufacturer H&R Johnson. 'Liqueur Bottles' (opposite), 'Two Fish' and 'Starflower' (above) and 'Four Fish' (right) were intended to be randomly placed among plain tiles. Kenneth Clark Pottery, London, England, *c.*1965

Overleaf These silkscreen-printed tiles were designed by Laurence Scarfe for Carter's. In the 1960s Scarfe began to produce more striking geometric patterns. Here we have a star pattern set into a square and placed centrally on a tile divided diagonally into black and white quadrants. Poole, Dorset, England, 1964

Opposite The Italian ceramic artist Pompeo Pianezzola began designing for commercial tile makers in the 1960s. Pianezzola continued a tradition of creating a pattern based on a square divided into multicoloured diagonals. Peggy Angus built on this patterning in the 1950s as did Laurence Scarfe in the 1960s (overleaf). Changing the orientation of each tile produced a variety of patterns over a large surface. Appiani Ceramics, Treviso, Italy, *c.*1973

Above The designer Laurence Scarfe exploded a six-pointed star, with inset rosette in a hexagon, to create a pattern of lively geometry. Two colours, blue and black, are silkscreened onto the tile in a way that cleverly reveals and incorporates into the design the creamy white ground glaze. Carter & Co., Poole, Dorset, England, 1964

Above Building on his 'star' pattern, Laurence Scarfe has created a stick-and-ball motif set within an octagon and with the points of the star distorted to the extent of becoming a pinwheel. Carter & Co., Poole, Dorset, England, 1964

Opposite Peggy Angus started producing geometric forms in the early 1950s. She revisited her 'star' designs in combination with geometric forms and in different media into the early 1980s. This design, screenprinted in peach on a creamy white ground, would have been used in conjunction with similarly patterned or plain-coloured tiles. Carter & Co., Poole, Dorset, England, 1950s

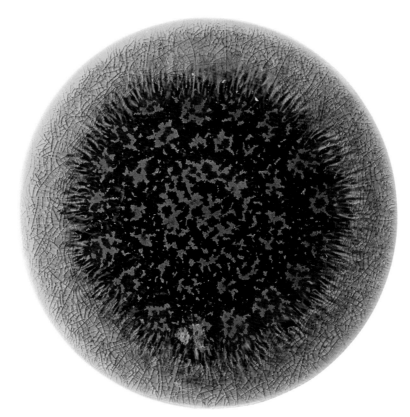

Opposite Peggy Angus stated that her favourite designs were the simplest units, like this circle. She created this tile design in conjunction with another consisting of two addorsed half circles. Placing the circles between the half circles over a large surface, formed a continuous wavy pattern. Carter & Co., Poole, Dorset, England, 1950s

Above This circular tile was screen printed in black glaze onto an unglazed tile, then oversprayed with a transparent turquoise glaze, creating a startling, crazed effect. It was designed by Ann Wynn Reeves in 1967 for use in doorbell sounding boxes for the English manufacturers of electrical fittings, V. & E. Friedland. Kenneth Clark Pottery, London, England, mid-1970s

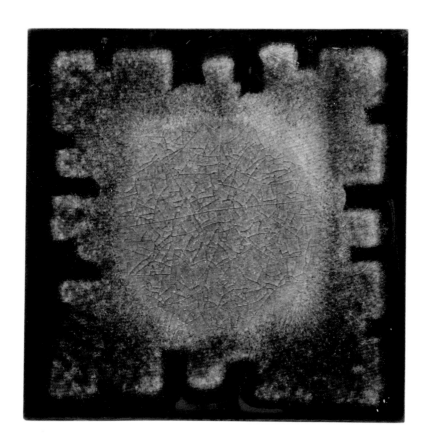

Above, opposite and overleaf These tiles are from the 'Summer Designs' range designed by Kenneth Clark in 1970. They are decorated with a combination of coloured transparent and semi-transparent glazes on coloured backgrounds and were intended to be used with plain colour-glazed tiles. Kenneth Clark Pottery, London, England, 1970s

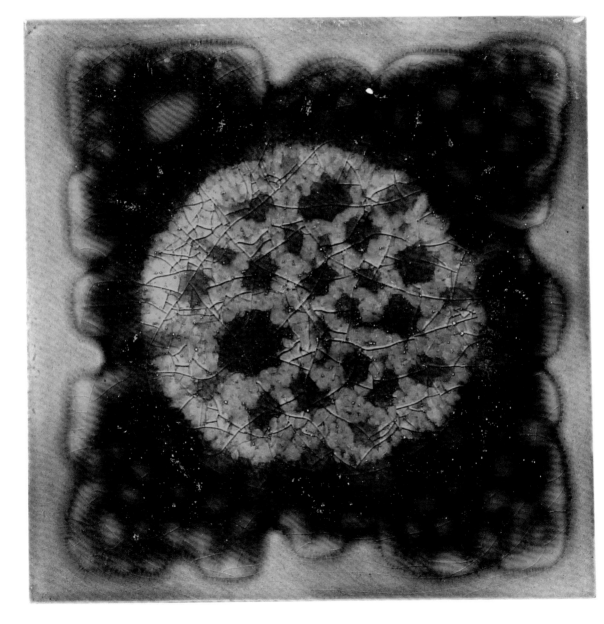

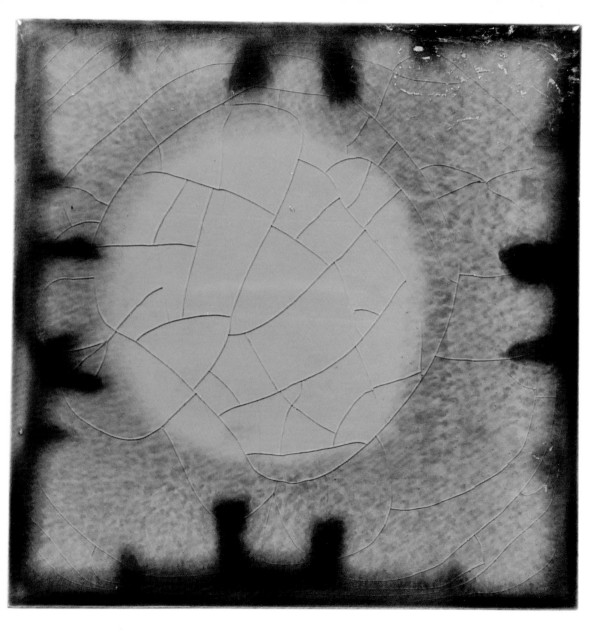

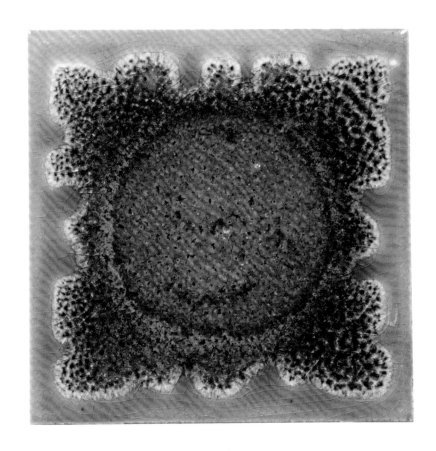

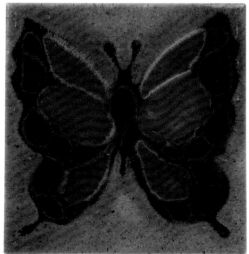
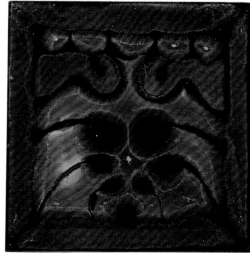

Above These tiles were designed and decorated by Ann Wynn Reeves in 1974. The pattern (a butterfly and an abstract) as well as the background was hand-trailed in different coloured glazes. These feature tiles were intended to be used with plain colour-glazed tiles. Kenneth Clark Pottery, London, England, *c.*1974

Opposite Ann and Kenneth Clark began making moulded tiles in the 1950s. Raw clay was pressed into a plaster mould and the resulting raised ridges served to contain hand-applied coloured glaze. The whole tile was then oversprayed with another transparent coloured glaze. This abstract tile was designed by Ann Wynn Reeves in 1968. Kenneth Clark Pottery, London, England, *c.*1968

Overleaf This multicoloured banded chevron pattern was designed for wall tiles in the Carter & Co. tearooms in Poole, Dorset. The bold but softly blurred spray-painted line pattern had an influence on later tile artists including Sally Anderson (following pages). This tile was designed by Reginald Till, *c.*1928, and adapted by Truda Carter, *c.*1930. Carter & Co., Poole, Dorset, England, *c.*1930

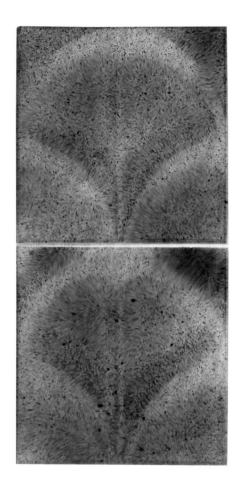

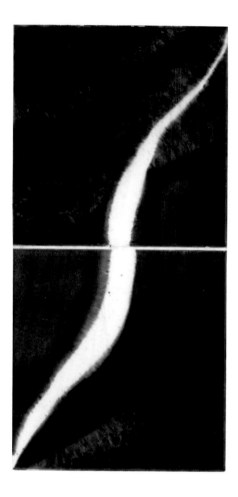

Above and opposite These four different designs are part of the 'One Step On' range of wall tiles by the tile artist Sally Anderson. She encouraged her clients to form their own repeating patterns, using single tiles in different orientations within each range. Entitled 'Plumage', 'Tiderace', 'Rainstorm' and 'Wych Elm', these four designs were inspired by nature and produced in 25 different colour ways. Sally Anderson (Ceramics) Ltd, Harlow, Essex, England, *c*.1976

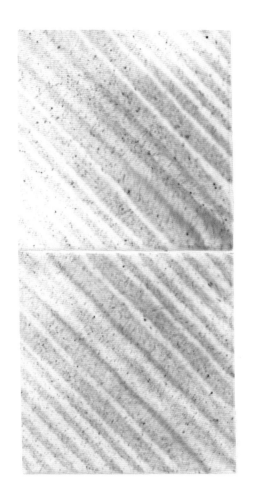

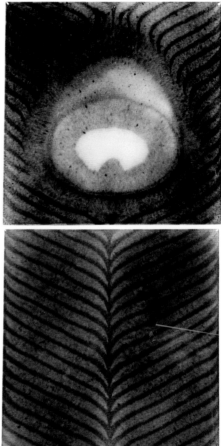

Above and opposite Sally Anderson produced this 'Peacock' design, also from the 'One Step On' range of wall tiles, in four different colour ways. She modified contemporary screenprinting practices to achieve a more evenly distributed glaze.

This range won the 1976 Design Council Award and was shown in 'The Way We Live: Design for Interiors, 1950 to the Present Day' exhibition at the Victoria and Albert Museum in 1978. Harlow, Essex, England, *c.*1976

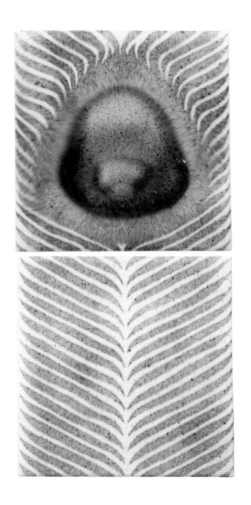
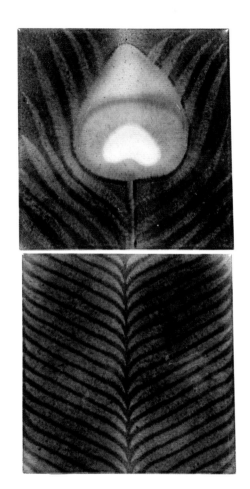

Above and opposite In 1974 the Design Council presented an award to Tarquin Cole and Rye Pottery for 'innovation, fitness for purpose, ease of use and good appearance'. The tiles above and opposite are from the 'Blazer' range, consisting of square white glazed tiles with one or two enamel colour silkscreen-printed border stripes. Rye Pottery, Rye, East Sussex, England, 1973

Overleaf The 'Honeycomb' and 'Kensington' ranges of hexagonal tiles have two or three colours printed on a white or coloured glaze. All the tiles were designed by Tarquin Cole in 1973. Rye Pottery, Rye, East Sussex, England, 1973

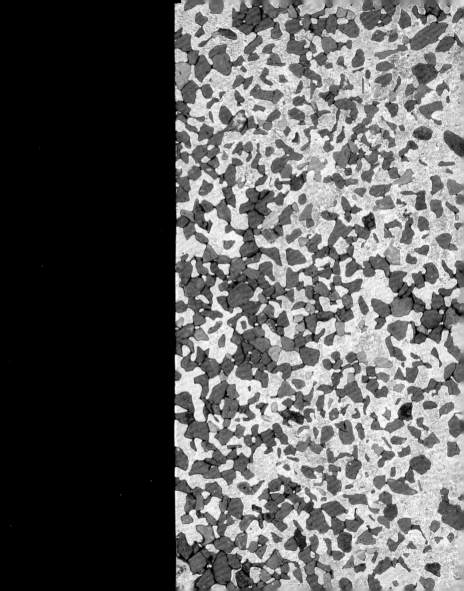

Previous pages Established by American designers
Thomas Schmidt and Jeffrey Stephen Miller, Recycled
China produces architectural components, artworks
and objects from discarded waste materials. The tile on
p.292 is made of blue-and-white porcelain fragments and
aluminium, while the tile on p.293 is constructed out of
red brick fragments and aluminium. Beijing, China, 2014

Above and opposite Egyptian ceramic artist Diaa el-Din
Daoud is inspired by the landscape, especially of the Siwa
Oasis in the Western Desert. The colours of his tile panel
evoke the sand, sky and water, while the incised lines
reflect embroidery designs on the traditional costume
that women wear in that region. Fustat, Egypt, 2018

GLOSSARY

Arista or press-moulded tiles are made by pressing clay against a mould. The raised borders of the design prevent the applied colours from running together during firing. Also known as the *cuenca* technique.

Block-printing is a method of creating a design on a ceramic tile by use of a carved or formed block prepared with ink or paint.

Chromolithography is a method for transferring an image from a flat piece of stone (lithography) to create colour prints.

Cuerda seca is a technique used to separate coloured glazes on the surface of a tile. A thin line of dark pigment mixed with grease or wax is used to outline the borders of the design, preventing the coloured glazes from running together during firing.

Delftware is a term for painted tin-glazed earthenware made in the Netherlands and in England. This product became associated with the city of Delft in the 17th century but was made in other Dutch centres as well.

Dust-pressed tiles are created by pressing clay power into moulds at high pressures. As these types of tiles require minimal drying, the technique lends itself to mass production. Relief-decorated tiles are made with metal dies.

Earthenware is a common type of potter clay fired at a relatively low temperature. It is often covered with a glaze for decoration and to render it impervious to liquids.

Faience (fayence) is a term arising in the 16th century for painted tin-glazed earthenware made in France, Germany and Scandinavia. The term may be derived from the name of the city of Faenza, where many Italian maiolica ceramics were exported throughout Europe.

Fritware pottery combines frit (ground glass) with clay to reduce the temperature required for firing and produces a strong white body that approximates the result of porcelain.

Inlaid tiles are made by combining at least two colours of clay to create a pattern. The pattern is created with a stamp, which has been carved in relief, or by pressing into a mould; the depressions are then filled with either solid clay or clay in slip form.

Lustreware is painted tin-glazed earthenware with additional decoration executed with metal oxides and fired in a reduced atmosphere, creating a shiny metallic film.

Maiolica is a term for painted tin-glazed earthenware produced in Italy from the 13th century. The technique was introduced by Italian shipping merchants from Islamic pottery centres in the western Mediterranean.

Majolica is a general term for ceramics that are decorated with coloured lead glazes.

Pouncing is a technique used to transfer patterns. The outline of the design is drawn on paper and then pricked through with a pin. Crushed charcoal is then 'pounced' through these holes using a small bag (or 'pounce'), leaving a pattern of dots to guide the painter.

Saz leaf design is a 16th-century Ottoman design motif of a twisting serrated leaf.

Sgraffito is a technique in which a design is incised through a coating of a different colour slip, glaze or pigment, revealing the clay surface underneath.

Slip is clay watered down to a creamy consistency.

Slip trailing (or tube-lining) is a technique in which lines of clay slip are applied to the surface of a ceramic object, often through a nozzle.

Stencilling is a method for executing a design onto a ceramic by the use of a pre-cut pattern.

Tin-glazed earthenware has been covered with a white opaque glaze, specifically a lead glaze opacified by the addition of tin oxide. It is variously called faience, fayence, maiolica or delftware.

Transfer-printing is a way of reproducing two-dimensional designs onto ceramics. A design is printed onto a sheet of tissue paper or a thin gelatinous layer and then transferred onto the ceramic.

Tube-lining *see* slip trailing.

FURTHER READING

Arber, Katie, *Patterns for Post-war Britain: The Tile Designs of Peggy Angus* (London, 2002)

Archer, Michael, *Delftware* (London, 1997)

Atasoy, Nurhan and Julian Raby, *Iznik: The Pottery of Ottoman Turkey* (London, 1994)

Atterbury, Paul and Clive Wainwright, *Pugin: A Gothic Passion* (New Haven and London, 1994)

Austwick, J. and B. Austwick, *The Decorated Tile* (London, 1980)

Beaulah, Kenneth and Hans Van Lemmen, *Church Tiles of the Nineteenth Century* (London, 2001)

Betts, Ian M. and Rosemary I. Weinstein, *Tin-Glazed Tiles from London* (London, 2010)

Blanchett, Chris, *20th Century Decorative British Tiles* (Pennsylvania, 2005)

Eames, Elizabeth, *English Tilers* (London, 1992)

— *English Medieval Tiles* (London, 1985)

Canby, Sheila R. and Arthur Millner, *Damascus Tiles: Mamluk and Ottoman Architectural Ceramics from Syria* (New York and London, 2015)

Carey, Moya, *Persian Art: Collecting the Arts of Iran in the 19th Century* (London, 2017)

Carter C. and H.R. Hidden, *Wall and Floor Tiling* (London, 1951)

Clark, Kenneth, *The Tile: Making, Designing and Using* (Marlborough, 2002)

Corbett, Angela and Corbett, Barry, *Tiles Tell the Tale* (Pilkington's Lancastrian Pottery Society, 2004)

Crumpton, Gillian (ed.), *The John Scott Tile Collection* (London, 2017)

Dam, Jan Daan van et al., *Dutch Tiles* (Philadelphia, 1984)

Denny, Walter B., *Iznik: The Artistry of Ottoman Ceramics* (London, 2004)

Embree, Sally and John Stewart, *Earth, Brick & Terracotta*, 2 vols (with a special chapter on tiles), (London, 2015)

Fawcett, Jane (ed.), *Historic Floors: Their History and Conservation* (Oxford, 1998)

Graves, Alun, *Tiles and Tilework of Europe* (London, 2002)

Guy, John, *Indian Temple Sculpture* (London, 2018)

Hamilton, D., *The Thames and Hudson Manual of Architectural Ceramics* (London, 1978)

Hayward, Leslie, *Poole Pottery: Carter & Company and their Successors, 1873–2002*, ed. Paul Atterbury (3rd edn: Shepton Beauchamp, 2002)

Hawkins, J., *The Poole Potteries* (London, 1980)

Herbert, Tony and Kathy Huggins, *The Decorative Tile* (London, 1995)

Jones, Joan, *Minton: The First Two Hundred Years of Design and Production* (Shrewsbury, 1993)

Lemmen, Hans van, *5,000 Years of Tiles* (London, 2013)

— *Art Deco Tiles* (London, 2012)

— *Delftware Tiles* (London, 2005)

— *Medieval Tiles* (London, 2004)

— *Tiles in Architecture* (London, 1993)

— *Victorian Tiles* (London, 2000)

Lemmen, Hans van and Chris Blanchett, *20th Century Tiles* (Princes Risborough, 1999)

Myers, Hilary and Richard Myers, *William Morris Tiles: The Tile Designs of Morris and his Fellow Workers* (Shepton Beauchamp, 1996)

Oney, Gonul, *Ceramic Tiles in Islamic Architecture* (Istanbul, 1987)

Pearson, Lynn, *Tile Gazetteer: A Guide to British Tile and Architectural Ceramics Locations* (Shepton Beauchamp, 2005)

Pereira, Joao Castel-Branco, *Portuguese Tiles from the National Museum of Azulejo, Lisbon* (Lisbon, 1999)

Pickett, Douglas, *Early Persian Tilework: The Medieval Flowering of Kashi* (Cranbury, London, Mississauga, 1997)

Porter, Venetia, *Islamic Tiles* (London, 1995)

Ray, Anthony, *English Delftware Tiles* (London, 1973)

— *Liverpool Printed Tiles* (London, 1994)

Riley, Noel, *Tile Art: A History of Decorative Ceramic Tiles* (London, 1987)

Rosser-Owen, Mariam, *Islamic Arts from Spain* (London, 2010)

Stanley, Tim, *Palace and Mosque: Islamic Art for the Middle East* (London, 2006)

PICTURE CREDITS

p.16 © Dean and Chapter of Westminster
p.17 © Massimo Santi/dreamstime.com
p.18 Photo DeAgostini/Getty Images
p.19 Lois GoBe/Alamy Stock Photo
p.20 Photo © Will Pryce
p.22 Martin Lehmann/Alamy Stock Photo
p.23 © Luc Boegly/Artedia/VIEW
p.25 Nikreates/Alamy Stock Photo
pp.28–9 From the series 1125 to DD-1892
pp.30–1 C.97 to O-1981
p.32 446:1 to 4-1905, C.347-1927, C.345-1927
p.33 444A to D-1905
pp.34–5 C.469, 470-1927
p.36 1330-1892
p.37 1310-1892
p.38 1423-1892
p.39 1713-1892
p.40 left to right, top to bottom 218-1902, 173-1902, 99-1902, 201-1902, 213-1902, 98A-1902
p.41 150-1902
p.42 C.962-1922, C.963-1922
p.43 1714-1892
pp.44–5 Given by J.H. Fitzhenry, Esq., 1551-1903
p.46 1527-1876
p.47 71-1885
p.48 left 1485-1876
p.48 right Salting Bequest, 1841-1876
p.49 Salting Bequest, C.1976-1910
p.50 2054-1899
p.51 above 574 to B-1900
p.51 below 584 to C-1900
p.52 1025-1892
p.53 1892 to C/2-1897
pp.54-55 1837-1876
pp.56–7 left to right, top to bottom 113-1895, 559-1900, 1493-1876, 1493D-1876, 558-1900, 1836-1876, 592-1890
pp.58–9 514:1 to 40-1888
pp.60–1 left to right 412-1898, 411-1898, 503-1900

p.62 382-1894
p.63 607A, 608A, 609, 610E-1893, 6-1908
pp.64–5 229-1902
pp.68–9 966 to 980-1892, 992-1903
pp.70–1 4915 to 5386-1857
pp.72–3 30-1866
pp.74–5 8533-1863
p.76 9363:42/(IS)
p.77 clockwise from top left 9363:6/(IS), 9363:29/(IS), 9592(IS)
p.78 IM.565:7-1924
p.79 9363:56/(IS)
pp.80–1 1767 and 1766-1892
pp.82–3 From the series 605, 605A, 606-1893
pp.84–5 308:121, 154, 146-1866
pp.86–7 98J and K-1881, 96:4 to 5-1881, 97:6-1881
pp.88–9 1104, A-1905
p.90 498-1868
p.91 233-1893, 231-1893
p.92 595-1872
p.93 4780-1901, 2992-1853
pp.94–5 667-1897
p.96 430 to D-1900
p.97 428-1900
pp.98–9 401:1 to 24-1900
p.100 1889:1 to 16-1897
p.101 1886:1 to 8-1897
p.102 left to right, top to bottom 396-1905, C.14-1953, C.4-1953, 1020-1892
p.103 1680-1892
pp.104–5 908 to F-1894, 894-1897
pp.108–9 1427:1 to 27-1902
p.110 4:1 to 9-1897
p.111 129-1897
pp.112–13 345:1 to 29-1896
pp.114–5 306, 307-1879
pp.116–17 139:1 to 4-1891
pp.118–9 IS.52, A-1898
p.120 IS.62-1898
p.121 IM.244-1923, IM.247-1923
p.122 IM.269, 270, 272 and 273-1923
p.123 Circ.1295-1923, IM.263, 265 and 266-1923
p.124 left to right, top to bottom Given by Mr Henry Van der Bergh through Art Fund Circ. 130-1928, Circ.132-1928, CIRC.109-1928, 426:3-1905; C.499:4-1923
p.125 Given by Mr Henry Van der Bergh through Art Fund, C.498-1923

pp.216–19 Victoria and Albert Museum,
    Fabric of the Building Collection
p.220 512-1889
p.221 623-1868
p.222 230-1887
p.223 228-1887
pp.224–5 560-1888
pp.226–7 3-1877
pp.228–9 Given by Fortes (Holdings) Ltd,
    C.80C to E-1969
pp.230–1 C.15-1971
pp.232–3 C.189-1976
pp.234–5 C.67 and A-1980
pp.236–7 C.186E, O-1976
pp.238–9 C.173 to D-1976
pp.242–3 Given by Pilkington's Tile and Pottery Co.,
    309 to E-1903
pp.244–5 C.187 to F-1976
p.246 C.185C–1976
p.247 C.169 to C-1976
pp.248–9 Given by Susan Birch and Jennifer Opie,
    C.109-1980, C.55-2007
p.250 Given by Margaret Bully, MISC.2:112/7-1934
p.251 C.25-1998
p. 252 C.22-1999 (mid 1920s), © Estate Of Vanessa Bell,
    courtesy of Henrietta Garnett
p.253 MISC.2:62-1934 © Estate of Duncan Grant.
    All rights reserved, DACS 2019
pp.254–5 Given by the British Institute of Industrial Art,
    C.11-1978 © The Estate of Edward Bawden
pp. 256–7 Given by London Transport, C.30-1979,
    C.3-1997, C.32-1979, C.31-1979
pp.258 C.48-1946 © The Bernard Leach Family.
    All rights reserved, DACS 2019
p.259 C.193:5-1985
p.260-1 left to right C.67-1979, C.71-1979 © Estate of
    Peggy Angus. All Rights Reserved, DACS 2019;
    C.73-1979 © Victoria Gibson; C.70-1979 © Estate
    of Peggy Angus. All Rights Reserved, DACS 2019
pp.262–3 C.72 and C.74-1979 Designed by Peggy Angus
    & Victoria Gibson © Victoria Gibson and the Estate
    of Peggy Angus
pp.264–5 Given by Kenneth Clark Pottery, C.159, B to
    C-1980 © Estate of the Artist and Jenna Burlingham
    Fine Art
pp.266–7 Given by Kenneth Clark Pottery, C.158
    to C-1980 © Ann Wynn Reeves for Kenneth
    Clark Pottery

pp.268–9 C.311-1978 © Estate of the Artist
    and Jenna Burlingham Fine Art
p.270 C.29-1982
p.271 C.31D-1978 © Estate of the Artist and
    Jenna Burlingham Fine Art
p.272 C.31H-1978 © Estate of the Artist and
    Jenna Burlingham Fine Art
p.273 C.69-1979 © Estate of Peggy Angus.
    All Rights Reserved, DACS 2019
p.274 C.68-1979 © Estate of Peggy Angus.
    All Rights Reserved, DACS 2019
p.275 Given by Kenneth Clark Pottery, C.160-1980
    © Ann Wynn Reeves for Kenneth Clark Pottery
p.276-9 Given by Kenneth Clark Pottery, C.161 to C-1980
    © Kenneth Clark Pottery
p.280 Given by Kenneth Clark Pottery, C.164A-1980,
    C.164-1980 © Ann Wynn Reeves for Kenneth Clark
    Pottery
p.281 Given by Kenneth Clark Pottery, C.167-1980
    © Kenneth Clark Pottery
pp.282-3 C.200-1977
pp.284–5 Given by Sally Anderson Ceramics,
    Left to right Circ.32,37,39 and 35-1977
pp.286–7 Given by Sally Anderson Ceramics,
    Circ.109 to L-1979
p.288 C.188-1984 © Rye Pottery
p.289 C.197-1984 © Rye Pottery
pp.290–1 C.194, 190, 192, 191-1984 © Rye Pottery
pp.292–3 Given by Recycled China (Thomas Schmidt
    and Jeffrey Stephen Miller), FE.53 and 54-2015
    © Recycled China/ Jeffrey Stephen Miller and
    Thomas Schmidt
pp.294–5 ME.14-2019 © Diaa el-Din Daoud

INDEX

Page numbers in *italics* refer to illustrations

ACKNOWLEDGMENTS

The publishers would like to thank everyone who contributed to the research, writing and production of this book. In particular, we would like to acknowledge the expertise and unfaltering enthusiasm of Terry Bloxham, without whom this book would not have been possible. Many thanks also go to the many curators at the Victoria and Albert Museum who advised on and researched the selection of tiles included in this book, notably Nick Barnard, Fuchsia Hart, Alun Graves, Tim Stanley and Susan Stronge, with special thanks to Mariam Rosser-Owen for her continued support. We are also very grateful to Caroline Brooke Johnson for her excellent work as copy-editor and are indebted to the team at Here Design for the original concept and design, most notably Alex Merrett and Sam White.

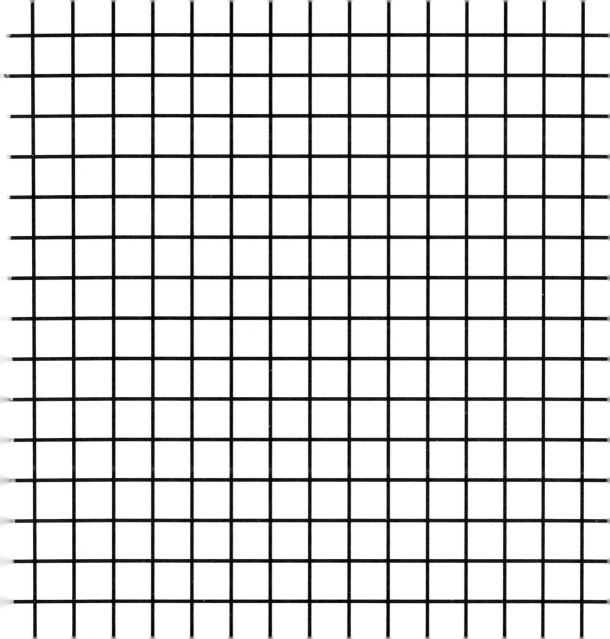

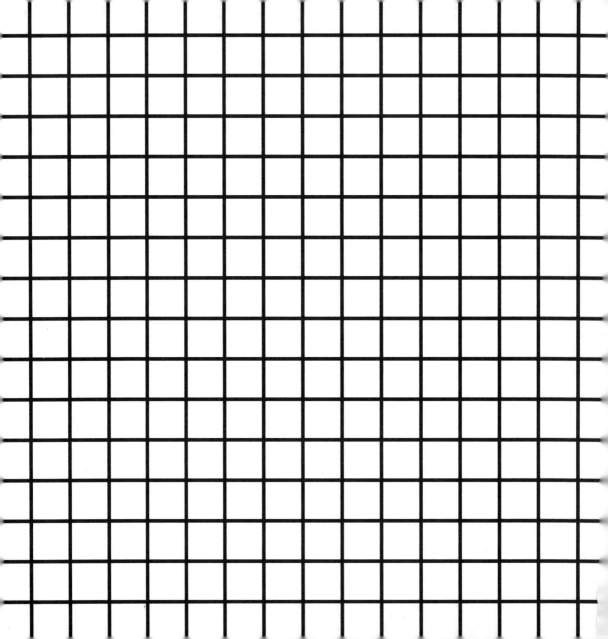